57306283

What Is Anxiety Disorder?

Other titles in the *Understanding Mental Disorders* series include:

What Are Sleep Disorders?
What Is Bipolar Disorder?
What Is Panic Disorder?
What Is Schizophrenia?
What Is Self-Injury Disorder?

UNDERSTANDING
MENTAL DISORDERS

What Is Anxiety Disorder?

Carla Mooney

ReferencePoint
Press®

San Diego, CA

For more information, contact:
ReferencePoint Press, Inc.
PO Box 27779
San Diego, CA 92198
www.ReferencePointPress.com

LIBRARY OF CONGRESS CATALOGING-IN-PUBLICATION DATA

Mooney, Carla, 1970-
  What is anxiety disorder? / by Carla Mooney.
      pages cm. -- (Understanding mental disorders)
  Includes bibliographical references and index.
  ISBN-13: 978-1-60152-920-6 (hardback)
  ISBN-10: 1-60152-920-1 (hardback)
  1. Anxiety disorders--Juvenile literature. 2. Anxiety disorders--Treatment--Juvenile literature.
I. Title.
  RC531.M65 2016
  616.85'22--dc23
                                                              2015016548

CONTENTS

INTRODUCTION

Gripped by Fear

One morning in San Francisco, twenty-five-year-old Richard Lucas headed to work. Following his usual routine, he stopped along the way for breakfast and then sat outside his office to smoke a cigarette. Then suddenly, he was gripped by pain. He describes the feeling: "Suddenly and inexplicably, pain covered my chest. Squeezing pain, as if someone had picked me up from behind and given me a bear hug of massive proportions. I stood up, stretched and rubbed my chest, hoping for the pain to disperse. But it got worse."[1]

Lucas hoped the pain would go away, and he went into his office and sat down. Noticing that Lucas was visibly uncomfortable, his boss asked if he was okay. When Lucas described his symptoms, his boss suggested that he go to the hospital. Certain that he was having a heart attack, Lucas agreed.

Symptoms Caused by Stress

When Lucas arrived at the hospital's emergency room, nurses and doctors rushed him to an exam room, where they ran multiple tests. After several hours of testing, the results showed that Lucas was not having a heart attack. In fact, there was nothing physically wrong with him. Instead, the doctors said his symptoms were caused by stress. Lucas was shocked by this. "I was utterly dumbfounded by the idea that I, always fearless and never really worried about anything, could have been reduced to a blubbering victim of stress," he says. "It made no sense."[2] At the same time, Lucas was relieved that he was not dying and that the doctor's examination had not found any medical problems. He was ready to put the incident behind him and move forward with his life.

Yet on a business trip a few weeks later, the severe chest pain struck Lucas again. Once again he went to the hospital's emergency room, where doctors told him that stress was the cause of his pain. Over the next five years, Lucas continued to experience what he later learned were panic attacks. He visited the emergency room twenty-five times and developed a constant fear that an attack would strike at any minute. "I checked my pulse constantly to make sure my heart was still beating," he says. "I lay in bed with my hand on my chest to feel my heart, and I went into panic mode daily."[3]

Eventually, Lucas found a doctor who helped him treat his anxiety with medication and therapy. Although he still struggles with anxiety, Lucas has learned to manage his disorder and has not been back to the emergency room for a panic attack in months. He is also revisiting hobbies that his anxiety made impossible to pursue. For example, before his disorder set in, Lucas was a scuba instructor who navigated

> "Suddenly and inexplicably, pain covered my chest. Squeezing pain, as if someone had picked me up from behind and given me a bear hug of massive proportions."[1]
>
> —Richard Lucas, anxiety disorder sufferer.

A young man clutches his chest in pain. Chest pain is a common symptom of anxiety that may be mistaken for a heart attack by the person experiencing it.

the ocean depths with his students. After having a panic attack during a dive, however, Lucas stopped. "In a few months I will return to the depths of the ocean and I will conquer my fear," he vows. "I will not allow anxiety and panic to kill another day of my life. It's my life, and anxiety can't have it anymore."[4]

Anxiety: A Serious Mental Illness

Fear and anxiety are normal emotions. But when anxiety persists and worsens over time, a person may have an anxiety disorder. Anxiety disorders are a group of serious mental illnesses. Like Lucas experienced, anxiety may cause physical symptoms such as chest pains or nightmares. Sometimes, anxiety can get so bad that it interferes with a person's ability to lead a normal life.

> "I will not allow anxiety and panic to kill another day of my life. It's my life, and anxiety can't have it anymore."[4]
>
> —Richard Lucas, anxiety disorder sufferer.

People who suffer from an anxiety disorder are not alone. Anxiety disorders are the most common mental illness; the Anxiety and Depression Association of America (ADAA) estimates that approximately 40 million adults in the United States are affected. Anxiety can affect anyone, rich or poor, young or old. In fact, many prominent Americans have suffered from an anxiety disorder. In 2012 singer LeAnn Rimes entered an inpatient treatment facility for severe anxiety and stress. Many historians believe that President Abraham Lincoln suffered from generalized anxiety disorder. Legendary singer Barbra Streisand developed social anxiety disorder and stopped performing for the general public for years.

There is hope for people who struggle with anxiety disorders. With treatment, sufferers can learn to manage the disorder and its symptoms and lead a normal, productive, and satisfying life.

CHAPTER 1

What Is Anxiety Disorder?

Everyone feels anxious sometimes. Modern life is full of stressful situations, deadlines, and demands. People worry about tests and responsibilities. They worry they have lost their keys, forgotten to lock their door, or left their iron turned on. Feeling anxious is a normal reaction to stressful situations and can even be a helpful emotion. Mild anxiety and stress can help people perform under pressure and tighten their focus when studying or handling an important event.

Anxiety is also the body's natural response to danger; it is the alarm that sounds when a person feels threatened. This response can help someone react appropriately to danger by triggering a fight-or-flight stress response, a physiological reaction to a dangerous situation that prepares the body to either stay and fight or flee. In this way anxiety can help a person stay focused, leap into action, or solve a critical problem.

Most of the time feelings of anxiety disappear soon after the situation that caused them is over. In some cases, however, feelings of anxiety can become excessive and worsen over time. Some people develop an irrational fear of everyday situations and feel anxious even when there is no real threat or danger present. They may have chest pains or nightmares and have trouble with normal daily tasks. They can become paralyzed by inaction and withdraw from family and friends. For these people anxiety is constant and overwhelming. It interferes with their relationships and activities. In these cases anxiety has become a disabling mental disorder.

Signs and Symptoms

Anxiety disorders are a group of mental illnesses that cause abnormal feelings of fear and dread. These feelings may be caused by a fear of a specific object or situation, such as snakes, crowds, taking tests, or even something as small as a pencil or piece of dirt. Alternatively, the fear may be more general and all-encompassing. The word *anxiety* comes from the Greek root that means "to press tight" or "to strangle." True to this definition, many people who suffer from an anxiety disorder report feeling as if they are being strangled by their fear.

Anxiety disorders are different from normal, routine feelings of anxiety. A person with a disorder experiences anxiety that is more intense, lasts longer, and leads to phobias that disrupt everyday routines. If anxiety symptoms last at least six months, a person may be suffering from a disorder. Without treatment, symptoms can worsen over time.

There are several types of anxiety disorders, each with its own signs and symptoms. The way each person experiences an anxiety disorder can be uniquely individual. One person may become anxious on an airplane, whereas another panics at the thought of going to a party with strangers. Other people experience overwhelming anxiety over driving, whereas others worry about germs and contamination.

Although anxiety disorders can take different forms and have all kinds of symptoms, all sufferers experience overwhelming and irrational feelings of fear and dread in situations that do not threaten most people. In addition, people who suffer from anxiety disorders often have several common symptoms, such as trouble concentrating or feeling tense, jumpy, restless, and irritable. Many people with an anxiety disorder feel like they have to constantly be on the watch for danger. Others feel as if their mind goes blank.

Anxiety disorders also cause physical symptoms. These include a pounding heart, sweating, stomach upset, dizziness, and frequent urination or diarrhea. Some people may experience shortness of breath, tremors, muscle tension, fatigue, and headaches. In some cases anxiety disorders can disrupt sleeping patterns and cause insomnia. Many people with anxiety mistake these symptoms for another medical condition, which may prompt them to visit a doctor. Once the doctor rules out a physical cause for their symptoms, they may be diagnosed with an anxiety disorder.

Anxiety Disorders More Common than Other Mood, Behavior Disorders in Teens

More teens are affected by anxiety than mood and behavior disorders. According to the Substance Abuse and Mental Health Services Administration (SAMHSA), anxiety disorders affect nearly one-third of all teens between the ages of thirteen and eighteen.

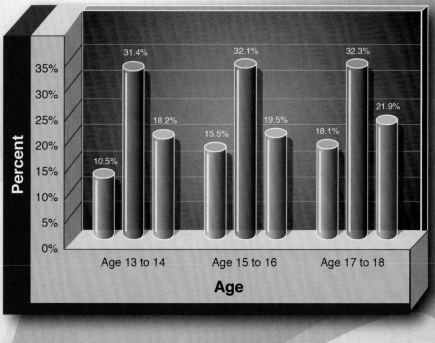

Mood disorders[1]　Anxiety disorders[2]　Behavior disorders[3]

[1] Mood disorders included disorders such as bipolar disorder and major depressive disorder.

[2] Anxiety disorders include disorders such as generalized anxiety and specific phobia.

[3] Behavior disorders such as attention-deficit/hyperactivity disorder, conduct disorder, and oppositional defiant disorder.

Source: Substance Abuse and Mental Health Services Administration, "Behavioral Health United States, 2012," 2013. p. 9. http://media.samhsa.gov.

Scott Stossel, editor of the *Atlantic* magazine, has suffered from anxiety for most of his life. At his wedding anxiety caused him to sweat so profusely that it soaked through his clothes. At the altar he trembled and shook so much that he had to lean on his wife for support.

When his first child was born, anxiety caused him to pass out, which forced the nurses to rush to him instead of tending to his wife, who was in labor.

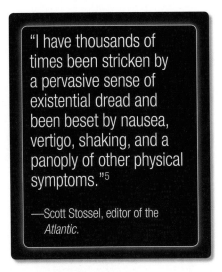

"I have thousands of times been stricken by a pervasive sense of existential dread and been beset by nausea, vertigo, shaking, and a panoply of other physical symptoms."[5]

—Scott Stossel, editor of the *Atlantic*.

Over the course of his life, anxiety has caused Stossel to skip dates and walk out of exams. He has anxiety attacks during job interviews, plane flights, train trips, and car rides. Even walking down the street can be a source of anxiety. "I have thousands of times been stricken by a pervasive sense of existential dread and been beset by nausea, vertigo, shaking, and a panoply of other physical symptoms," he says. "In these instances, I have sometimes been convinced that death, or something somehow worse, was imminent."[5] Sometimes, Stossel's anxiety causes stomachaches, headaches, dizziness, and arm and leg pain. Overall body aches can make him feel as if he has the flu. Anxiety can also make it difficult for him to breathe and swallow.

Who Is at Risk?

Anxiety disorders are the most common mental illnesses in the United States. According to the National Institute of Mental Health (NIMH), anxiety disorders affect about 40 million Americans over age eighteen per year, about 18 percent of the population. Anxiety disorders can strike people of any age, gender, race, or socioeconomic background.

Some factors can put a person at a greater risk of developing an anxiety disorder. According to the NIMH, women are 60 percent more likely than men to experience an anxiety disorder over their lifetime. Age is also a risk factor; several types of anxiety disorders such as phobias, obsessive-compulsive disorder, and separation anxiety are more likely to develop in early childhood, whereas social phobia and panic disorder are more likely to develop in teens. Race can influence who develops anxiety disorders, with non-Hispanic blacks 20 percent and Hispanics 30 percent less likely to experience an anxiety disorder during their lifetimes than non-Hispanic whites, according to the NIMH. Experiencing a traumatic event can also increase a person's risk of developing an anxiety disorder, particularly for those who suffer from a type called post-traumatic stress disorder.

Certain medical conditions have been linked to an increased risk of anxiety disorders. People who suffer from migraines, obstructive sleep apnea, mitral valve prolapse, irritable bowel syndrome, chronic fatigue syndrome, and premenstrual syndrome have a greater likelihood of developing an anxiety disorder at some point during their lifetime.

Although there are many types of anxiety disorders, most can be grouped into five major categories, each of which has its own specific characteristics: generalized anxiety disorder, obsessive-compulsive disorder, panic disorder, post-traumatic stress disorder, and phobias. The symptoms of each can range from mild to extreme. In addition, a person suffering from one type of anxiety disorder can be affected by one or more additional disorders at the same time.

Separation Anxiety Disorder

Many young children cry when their parents leave them at day care or with a babysitter. But for some children, the anxiety over being separated from their parents can constitute a disorder.

Separation anxiety disorder almost always occurs in children, rather than adults. It may be diagnosed in children who are excessively anxious and upset over detaching from a family member or their home. They may become extremely worried something bad will happen to their loved one. Separation anxiety disorder can also cause children to fear being lost or kidnapped. They may refuse to go to school, to sleep anywhere but their home, or to participate in activities that take them away from their loved ones or home. Some children experience headaches, stomachaches, and nausea and may even vomit at the thought of being separated. In most cases separation anxiety disorder disappears as children get older. However, if left untreated, it can lead to other anxiety disorders.

Generalized Anxiety Disorder

The ADAA estimates that about 6.8 million American adults—3.1 percent of the population—suffer from generalized anxiety disorder (GAD). Women are twice as likely as men to be affected by GAD, which emerges gradually and often develops between childhood and middle age.

People with GAD are consumed with worry about everyday things, even when there is little or no reason to feel concern. They constantly fret about money, health, family, work, and other issues. They expect the worst and anticipate disasters. When their anxiety is mild, people with GAD go about their lives with minimal disruption. When their anxiety becomes severe, however, their worrying may interfere with even the simplest daily tasks.

For GAD sufferers, just the thought of getting through the day can create anxiety. Although they may recognize that their anxiety is abnormal and excessive, they are unable to stop worrying. They may have trouble falling asleep or may struggle with insomnia. They may suffer physical symptoms such as trembling, twitching, muscle tension, headaches, irritability, sweating, and lightheadedness. They often feel tired and find it difficult to concentrate. Some suffer from depression.

Kat Kinsman is the editor in chief at Tasting Table, a culinary website and newsletter. She has struggled with GAD since she was a child. Kinsman says that there is no pattern to when anxiety strikes her. She describes having GAD in the following way: "If depression is, as [British politician] Winston Churchill famously described, a 'black dog' that follows the sufferer around, anxiety is a feral cat that springs from nowhere, sinks its claws into skin and hisses invective until nothing else exists."[6] Kinsman says that sometimes her anxiety gets so bad that she cannot leave her house to run even a simple errand such as picking up cream for her coffee. She explains:

"If depression is, as [British politician] Winston Churchill famously described, a 'black dog' that follows the sufferer around, anxiety is a feral cat that springs from nowhere, sinks its claws into skin and hisses invective until nothing else exists."[6]

—Kat Kinsman, editor in chief at Tasting Table and a GAD sufferer.

The thought of leaving the cocoon of my apartment—my bedroom, even—just crushes my lungs and tightens my skin until it's hot to the touch. My hands bobble the outline of the lipstick I try to apply so I can masquerade as a functioning human person, and I have to wipe it off and start again. And maybe again. And then my dress needs ironing. And the dogs need water. And I should answer another work e-mail. Anything to keep me from having to walk to the door, open it and face the world. The coffee will have to be black that day.[7]

Kinsman admits that she cannot explain what exactly she is afraid of, but she describes it as a free-floating fear that consumes her. She also experiences painful physical symptoms, including stomach, head, and muscle aches; chronic insomnia; and exhaustion.

Obsessive-Compulsive Disorder

Sufferers of obsessive-compulsive disorder (OCD) have certain thoughts (obsessions) over and over again that cause them severe anxiety and distress. They may realize that their obsession does not make sense, but they cannot stop their real and intense feelings. Unlike other anxiety disorders, OCD affects men and women in equal numbers, though every person experiences OCD differently.

In an attempt to control their obsessions, people with OCD feel an overwhelming urge to act out certain rituals or routines (compulsions). They repeatedly perform these compulsions to reduce the anxiety caused by their obsessions. For example, a person obsessed with symmetry may have a compulsion to organize and reorganize objects until they are arranged perfectly. A person obsessed with intruders may lock and relock windows and doors over and over each night. Others might feel compelled to touch objects in a specific order or to count things. People with OCD become consumed by their rituals even though they may recognize their senselessness.

If left untreated, the thoughts and behaviors of OCD may take over a person's life and interfere with their daily activities. For example, suppose a woman with OCD cannot stop thinking about germs, and she feels severe anxiety as a result. To reduce this anxiety, she might create a ritual to wash her hands repeatedly. Each time

she performs the washing ritual, her anxiety is temporarily lessened. Even so, the act of performing the ritual gives her no pleasure. She feels stuck in the routine and feels compelled to continue it, even if her skin becomes raw and bleeds from over-washing.

Panic Disorder

The ADAA reports that panic disorder affects about 6 million American adults. People who have panic disorder typically suffer through repeated panic attacks, which are episodes of intense panic or fear. Sometimes these episodes can be triggered by a particular situation, such as giving a speech to large group of people. In many cases, however, panic attacks strike without warning.

During a panic attack, individuals may feel intense terror. They usually experience heart palpitations and chest pains that are so intense they think they are having a heart attack. Others have trouble breathing, hyperventilate, or feel like they are choking. Those in the middle of a panic attack may experience hot flashes or chills, tremble or shake, or feel like they are going to throw up. The attacks and symptoms usually peak within ten minutes and rarely last more than thirty minutes.

Journalist Lee Kynaston suffers from panic disorder. His first attack took him completely by surprise. One night in 1997 he went to a restaurant with friends. After the waiter delivered his bowl of spaghetti, panic struck. Overwhelmed by a sudden, irrational fear, he ran outside, crouched on the street, and began to sweat, tremble, and hyperventilate. "All I knew is that I had to flee," he says. "My sudden exit may have been irrational, but it felt involuntary and instinctive. Once outside, I found myself dizzy, disorientated and disassociated. I was struggling for breath. I thought I was dying."[8]

Many people experience a panic attack or two during their lifetime, with no lasting consequences. For others, the experience of having a panic attack can cause significant anxiety about having future ones. People who develop panic disorder experience repeated attacks, though their frequency varies from person to person. Some people have panic attacks every week over a period of months. Others have clusters of daily attacks and then go through periods of remission.

> "Once outside, I found myself dizzy, disorientated and disassociated. I was struggling for breath. I thought I was dying."[8]
>
> —Lee Kynaston, a journalist who has panic disorder.

Regardless of how often attacks strike, sufferers worry constantly about having another one. To avoid another attack, sufferers will frequently change their behavior. They may stop going to places or avoid putting themselves in situations where previous attacks occurred. They may think that if they avoid the site of a previous panic attack, they can avoid having another one.

Post-Traumatic Stress Disorder

The ADAA estimates that approximately 7.7 million Americans age eighteen and older have post-traumatic stress disorder (PTSD).

PTSD is a type of anxiety disorder that results from experiencing a life-threatening or traumatic event. Although not every person who experiences a traumatic event will develop PTSD, for some the traumatic event triggers a severe and persistent emotional reaction. The events that trigger PTSD are typically violent and involve deliberate and destructive behavior, including war, sexual assaults, accidents, natural disasters, or the unexpected death of a loved one. In some cases PTSD occurs in people with serious illness or in people who have close friends and family dealing with serious illness. Mass violence is the most significant trigger for PTSD; according to the ADAA, 67 percent of people exposed to mass violence develop PTSD.

Although the events that trigger PTSD are different for each person, the symptoms of the disorder are similar. People with PTSD usually relive the traumatic event. They can have recurrent images, thoughts, flashbacks, dreams, or feelings of distress that remind them of the event in sharp detail. To escape the pain of remembering, they may avoid things that remind them of the trauma, including places, people, or objects. This avoidance may cause an emotional numbness, so that they feel dazed and have trouble remembering important details about the trauma. People who struggle with PTSD often experience an increased awareness of danger. They may become sleepless, irritable, startle easily, or appear to be hypervigilant of unknown dangers. PTSD symptoms can begin immediately after the triggering event or may emerge well after the event is over.

David Morris is a former marine infantry officer who suffers from PTSD. He served in the US Marine Corps and as a reporter in Iraq, where one day, while in southern Baghdad, he was nearly killed by an improvised explosive device. The memories of that experience continued to haunt him well after he was safe at home, and in the strangest of places. He recalls one time when he went to see a movie with his girlfriend and suddenly blacked out. "When I regained consciousness, I was pacing the lobby of the theater, looking at people's hands to make sure they weren't carrying weapons," he remembers. "Afterward, I asked my girlfriend what happened. 'There was an explosion in the movie,' she said. 'You got up and ran out.'"[9]

Suffering from PTSD incapacitated P.K. Phillips for more than thirty years. A beautiful and talented young woman who had a prom-

Soldiers who have experienced the horrors of war are among those who can suffer from post-traumatic stress disorder, or PTSD. Symptoms of the disorder include flashbacks to the stressful event, nightmares, and panic attacks.

ising career as a model ahead of her, Phillips endured a horrific trauma as a child in which she was sexually assaulted at knifepoint. "For months after the attack, I couldn't close my eyes without envisioning the face of my attacker," she writes. Unable to sleep alone in her house, for many years she obsessively checked that her doors and windows were locked, and she had panic attacks that made her unable to leave home. As a result, she had to end her modeling career.

Phillips would go through periods in which she felt better, but even decades after the attack, something would trigger her PTSD and send her reeling. "It was as if the past had evaporated, and I was back in the place of my attack," she writes. "I often felt disoriented, forgetting where, or who, I was. I would panic on the freeway and became unable to drive, again ending a career. I felt as if I had completely lost my mind."[10] It was not until she was nearly forty years old that medication and therapy helped her conquer her PTSD and get on with her life.

Phobias

Many experts believe that phobias are the most common form of anxiety disorder. A phobia is an intense, unrealistic, or exaggerated fear of a specific object, activity, or situation. Some people are phobic of animals such as snakes, whereas others fear heights. Most phobias involve things that are of little real danger. Sometimes a person does not even need to be physically near the object to feel afraid. Simply seeing a picture of the object or thinking about it can trigger a reaction.

In some cases phobias can be mild and manageable. People might avoid the objects or situations of which they are afraid, but they can still control their fears and engage in normal activities. For others, severe phobias can trigger strong irrational reactions. People with severe phobias might go to extreme measures to avoid the objects or situations they fear, which often makes the phobias stronger. Although these individuals usually realize their phobia is excessive and nonsensical, they feel unable to stop it. Simply thinking about their phobia can cause anxiety.

Faryl Zaklin, a thirty-eight-year-old from San Diego, has emetophobia, a fear of vomit. She says that since childhood, she has avoided people in amusement parks, concerts, and on airplanes that she is afraid are about to throw up. She constantly assesses her surroundings for signs that someone is about to vomit. If she suspects someone is going to throw up, she leaps out of the way. "It's panic, it's almost painful," she says. "I don't know anything else that's ever given me that much fear."[11]

Phobias can develop at any age, but most appear during adolescence or early adulthood. They typically develop suddenly without any specific trigger and may arise in situations that did not cause anxiety in the past.

Specific Phobias, Social Phobias, and Agoraphobia

Because phobias can take so many forms, doctors have classified them into three main categories: specific phobias, social phobias, and agoraphobia. Specific phobias involve an irrational fear of specific

A Variety of Fears

Phobias come in many forms. Here are a few:

Ablutophobia—fear of bathing
Acrophobia—fear of heights
Agyrophobia—fear of crossing the street
Anthophobia—fear of flowers
Bibliophobia—fear of books
Coimetrophobia—fear of cemeteries
Consecotaleophobia—fear of chopsticks
Entomophobia—fear of insects
Hemophobia—fear of blood
Iatrophobia—fear of doctors
Numerophobia—fear of numbers
Pyrophobia—fear of fire
Sciophobia—fear of shadows
Technophobia—fear of advanced technology
Venustraphobia—fear of beautiful women
Xenophobia—fear of strangers
Zoophobia—fear of animals

objects or situations. The most common specific phobias are fear of animals, flying, heights, water, injections, public transportation, confined spaces, dentists, storms, tunnels, and bridges. Some people have phobias of nonthreatening objects such as balloons, costume characters, and even certain numbers. Confronting the phobia may trigger feelings of panic and anxiety, sweating, breathing difficulties, and an increased heartbeat.

Social phobia, also known as social anxiety disorder, causes a person to fear being publicly criticized, embarrassed, and humiliated. Some people fear speaking in public or undertaking any activity that makes them the center of attention. People with social phobia tend to be extremely shy and often avoid parties and group events. They may also avoid crowded public places like shopping malls, concerts, sporting events, buses, and trains.

Agoraphobia is a complex anxiety disorder in which people fear and avoid places or situations that make them feel trapped, out of control, and embarrassed. For example, an agoraphobic may become anxious about using public transportation. Unlike social phobics, who may fear a bus or subway train because of its crowds, agoraphobics are afraid they will not be able to escape or get help should an anxiety attack strike them while on the bus. People with agoraphobia may fear being in either open or enclosed spaces, standing in line, and especially crowded places. In severe cases agoraphobics may refuse to leave home.

People who suffer from agoraphobia, social phobia, PTSD, and other anxiety disorders are sometimes embarrassed to admit they have a problem, and many try to hide their fears and symptoms from others. However, anxiety disorders are a serious medical condition that often warrant medical attention and long-term support.

CHAPTER 2

What Causes Anxiety Disorder?

Anxiety disorders can affect people of any age, gender, race, or socioeconomic background. The causes of these mental illnesses are not fully understood, which makes it difficult to predict who will develop one. Most mental health experts believe anxiety disorders do not have a single cause, but rather result from a combination of biological, genetic, psychological, and environmental factors. "Anxiety problems are brought about by a variety of causes operating on numerous different levels: heredity, biology, family background and upbringing, conditioning, recent stressors, your self-talk and personal belief system, your ability to express feelings, and so on,"[12] says Edmund Bourne, a clinical psychologist who specializes in the treatment of anxiety disorders.

The presence of one or more risk factors, however, does not guarantee a person will develop an anxiety disorder; it only means he or she has an increased chance of doing so. Many people with risk factors for anxiety disorders never develop them, but the more risk factors a person has, the more likely he or she will become ill.

Gender

Women have twice the risk of developing most anxiety disorders, compared to men. The reason why women are more vulnerable to anxiety disorders is unclear. Some studies have shown that hormonal differences make women more vulnerable to anxiety. In a 2010 study funded by the NIMH, researchers discovered that the brains of male rats were better able to adapt to a key stress hormone called corticotrophin-releasing factor than female rats' brains, making the males less sensitive to stress. "Although more research is necessary to determine whether this translates to humans, these findings may help to explain why women are twice as vulnerable as men to many stress-related disorders,"[13] says Rita Valentino, a neuroscientist at the University of Pennsylvania.

In another 2010 study on rats, researchers from Florida State University found that the male hormone testosterone may have a protective effect against anxiety. "The fact that females do not have a lot of testosterone may put them at risk of developing anxiety disorders,"[14] says Mohamed Kabbaj, study researcher and associate professor in the Florida State University College of Medicine.

> "Anxiety problems are brought about by a variety of causes operating on numerous different levels: heredity, biology, family background and upbringing, conditioning, recent stressors, your self-talk and personal belief system, your ability to express feelings, and so on."[12]
>
> —Edmund Bourne, clinical psychologist.

Some people believe that environmental influences make women more likely to develop anxiety disorders. Michelle Craske, an anxiety expert at the University of California–Los Angeles, argues that the differences in how boys and girls are treated as children may influence anxiety disorder. She points out that research shows that up until age eleven, girls and boys are equally likely to develop an anxiety disorder. However, only a few years later, at age fifteen girls are six times more likely to have an anxiety disorder.

Craske says this difference may be due to how parents treat their children. "From a socialization angle, there's quite a lot of evidence that little girls who exhibit shyness or anxiety are reinforced for it, whereas little boys who exhibit that behavior might even be punished for it,"[15] says Craske. For example, when a girl falls and cries, she may be more likely to be hugged and comforted, whereas a boy may be more likely to be encouraged to be tough. By repeatedly having emotional behavior such as crying rewarded with hugs and kisses, over time the girls learn that they will be rewarded for emotional reactions. As they grow into teens, years of reinforcement may lead to girls be-

A teenage girl weeps as her mother looks on. Although boys and girls experience anxiety disorders at the same rate before puberty, teenage girls are six times more likely than teenage boys to have such a disorder. Scientists are unsure whether this discrepancy is due to hormonal or cultural influences or both.

ing more likely to react emotionally and anxiously to negative situations in the future.

In addition, some argue that women may experience higher rates of anxiety disorders because contemporary society often puts cultural pressure on women to meet other's needs before their own, which causes stress. Others suggest that women are more likely to be diagnosed with an anxiety disorder because they are more willing to report their symptoms to health care providers.

Forgotten Trauma

A traumatic or violent event is a well-known cause of PTSD. Research shows, however, that a stressful or traumatic event does not actually need to be remembered for it to cause PTSD. In 2014 researcher Michael Fanselow and his colleagues reported that adults who suffer from PTSD may not have any memory of a childhood trauma that occurred early in life, before the juvenile brain was able to recall memories.

To test their theory, the researchers conducted experiments on young rats whose brains were not old enough to form explicit memories. They exposed the rats to a session of unpredictable stress. Once the rats became adults, the researchers tested the animals for their memory of the stressful event and measured their fear response. The rats did not show any evidence of remembering the stress, but they did show an increase in anxiety-related behavior. "These data highlight the importance of the many ways in which the brain processes traumatic experiences," says John H. Krystal, chief of psychiatry at Yale–New Haven Hospital. Krystal hopes that more research into how the brain processes traumatic experiences will yield promising new treatments for PTSD and other anxiety disorders.

Quoted in Brain & Behavior Research Foundation, "Even 'Forgotten' Trauma May Trigger PTSD Symptoms in Adults," August 29, 2014. https://bbrfoundation.org.

Heredity

Research into anxiety disorders shows that they tend to run in families. People who have a close relative with an anxiety disorder have a higher chance of developing the disorder themselves. Studies have shown that if a parent has panic disorder, his or her children are several times more likely to develop the disorder than children of parents who do not have the illness. People are also more likely to develop GAD and OCD if a close relative has one of these disorders.

In 2008 researchers from the University of California–Los Angeles studied earthquake survivors to find out whether PTSD, anxiety, and depression run in families. The researchers followed two hundred survivors of a massive earthquake in Armenia that killed seventeen thousand people in 1988. The survivors were from twelve multigenerational families—grandparents, parents, children, and grandchildren—and suffered from varying degrees of PTSD, anxiety, and depression. Using statistical analysis to assess heritability of PTSD, anxiety, and depression symptoms, the researchers concluded that an individual's genetic makeup affected his or her likelihood of developing the disorders. Specifically, they found that 41 percent of the variation in PTSD symptoms was caused by genetic factors, and 66 percent of anxiety and 61 percent of depression symptoms were caused by genetic factors. Although researchers do not yet know which specific genes are involved in these disorders, a genetic link has been confirmed.

Researchers are also investigating how genes and OCD are linked. According to the National Alliance on Mental Illness, about 25 percent of people with OCD have a family member who also has the disorder. Because of the family connection, researchers believe that genes may play a role in who develops OCD. In 2003 a collaborative landmark study funded by the National Institutes of Health discovered that OCD has a hereditary component. They discovered a mutated serotonin transporter gene called hSERT in families with OCD. A second OCD-related gene mutation was linked to the severity of symptoms.

Researchers have even been able to zero in on which genes might be involved in causing OCD. In 2013 an international research consortium led by investigators at Massachusetts General Hospital and the University of Chicago confirmed the heritability of OCD and Tourette's syndrome (TS), a neurological disorder, and even pinpointed a specific chromosome, a thread-like structure inside a cell nucleus that contains an organism's DNA, as a cause of OCD. "Both TS and OCD appear to have a genetic architecture of many different genes—perhaps hundreds in each person—acting in concert to cause disease," says researcher Jeremiah Scharf. "We found that OCD heritability appears to be concentrated in particular chromosomes—particularly chromosome 15."[16]

In 2014 researchers with Johns Hopkins University announced that they had identified a genetic marker—an easily identifiable piece of genetic material—that may be associated with the development of

OCD. The researchers scanned the genomes of more than fourteen hundred people with OCD, along with those of more than one thousand close relatives of people with OCD. They identified a significant association for OCD patients near a gene called protein tyrosine phosphokinase. Scientists believe that this gene is involved in learning and memory, which are qualities that are also affected by OCD. The gene has also been associated with attention-deficit/hyperactivity disorder, which has some of the same symptoms as OCD. "We hope this interesting finding brings us closer to making better sense of [OCD]—and helps us find ways to treat it,"[17] says study leader Gerald Nestadt.

Still, scientists believe much work remains to understand how genes influence anxiety disorders. A single gene linked to anxiety disorders has not yet been found, though researchers suspect that several genes may work together to make a person more vulnerable to an anxiety disorder. At the same time, researchers believe that other factors such as environment, stress, and brain function also play a role in who develops anxiety.

Brain Structure: The Amygdala

The human brain controls basic emotions, including fear and anxiety. Scientists believe that differences in brain structure and function may play a role in who develops an anxiety disorder. Using sophisticated brain-imaging technology, researchers can look at a detailed image of the brain's parts and how they operate. This has enabled scientists to identify areas of the brain that are associated with anxiety responses, particularly the amygdala.

The amygdala is an almond-shaped structure located deep in the brain. Like many brain structures, there are two amygdalae, one in each brain hemisphere. The amygdala is thought to be a communications hub between different parts of the brain, acting as a relay station between the parts that receive sensory input and the parts that interpret the signals. The amygdala regulates fear, memory, and emotion. It coordinates these responses with heart rate, blood pressure, and other physical responses to stressful events. For this reason, the amygdala is sometimes called the brain's "fear center." Some studies have shown that in people with anxiety disorders, the amygdala is highly sensitive to new or unfamiliar situations and reacts with a high stress response. In addition, the amygdala stores some emotional memories and may be linked to anxiety disorders that center on specific phobias, such as a fear of dogs, spiders, or flying.

In 2013 researchers at the Stanford University School of Medicine reported that measuring the size and connectivity of the amygdala can help them predict the degree of anxiety a child experiences in his or her daily life. The researchers studied seventy-six children aged seven to nine. Parents completed a questionnaire to assess their child's general cognitive, social, and emotional well-being. Then researchers took pictures of the children's brains using magnetic resonance imaging (MRI), which produces a detailed picture of the brain, and functional magnetic resonance imaging (fMRI), which measures brain activity by detecting changes in blood flow. The researchers compared the questionnaires with MRI and fMRI scans that measured the size and connectivity of the children's amygdalae.

They found that the larger the amygdala and the stronger its connections to brain areas responsible for perception and regulation of emotion, the greater the anxiety a child experienced. Their findings supported earlier studies of adults that also showed enlarged, highly connected amygdalae in people with anxiety disorders. The researchers caution that not every child with an enlarged and highly connected amygdala will go on to develop an anxiety disorder. "But it is an important step in the identification of young children at risk for clinical anxiety,"[18] says Vinod Menon, senior author of the study.

How the Hippocampus May Influence Anxiety Disorders

The hippocampus is another area of the brain that may influence anxiety disorders. The hippocampus is a small area that is associated with storing and retrieving memories. It allows the brain to convert new information into long-term memories. Studies have shown that some people who have experienced violent events—such as victims of child abuse or soldiers who served in combat—are more likely to have a smaller hippocampus than those who have not. This may be due to the fact that when the body experiences ongoing stress, the stress

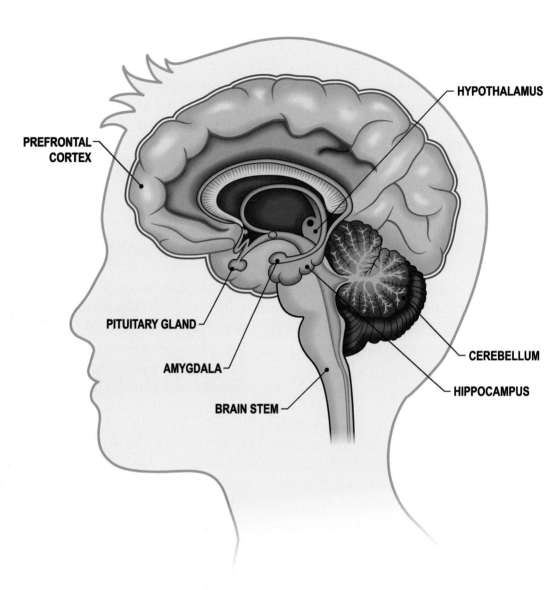

The amygdala and hippocampus are parts of the human brain that are associated with anxiety disorders. Studies have shown that people who experience trauma are more likely to have a smaller hippocampus than those who have not, and one study suggested that the size of the amygdala in children influences the level of anxiety they experience.

hormone cortisol affects the rate at which neurons are added to or subtracted from the hippocampus. When cortisol levels are increased for an extended period, it can cause the hippocampus to lose neurons and shrink in size. This restricts the brain's ability to take in new information and may be linked to the memory flashbacks and disruption experienced by patients with PTSD and other anxiety disorders.

Changes in brain structure and the connections between different areas of the brain may also be linked to OCD. Using sophisticated brain-imaging technology, researchers have found that people with OCD have abnormal activity in areas of the brain that are associated with anxiety, habit formation, and skill learning. In a 2008 study, for example, researchers at the University of Cambridge in England used fMRI technology to measure brain activity in the lateral orbitofrontal cortex, which is believed to be involved in decision making and behavior and may be important in stopping habitual behavior. The researchers reported that people with OCD and their family members showed underactivation in the lateral orbitofrontal cortex and other brain areas, which "probably predisposes [them] to developing the compulsive rigid symptoms that are characteristic of OCD,"[19] says Samuel Chamberlain, one of the study's researchers.

> "There are a lot of neuroimaging studies in OCD that suggest that the connections between regions of the brain are different in people who have OCD."[20]
>
> —Dorothy Grice, professor of psychiatry at Mount Sinai Hospital.

Some scientists believe that the repeated unpleasant thoughts and feelings of OCD may develop when there is a communication problem in different areas of the brain. "There are a lot of neuroimaging studies in OCD that suggest that the connections between regions of the brain are different in people who have OCD,"[20] says Dorothy Grice, a professor of psychiatry at Mount Sinai Hospital. She says that understanding the nuanced brains of people with anxiety disorder can help scientists develop targeted treatments.

Brain Chemistry

Studies suggest that brain chemistry may also play a role in the development of anxiety disorders. Neurotransmitters are chemicals in the brain that send signals across gaps called synapses between the brain's nerve cells. They affect how a person feels, thinks, and behaves. Research has shown that people with anxiety often have imbalances in certain neurotransmitters that can cause the brain's messages to be delivered incorrectly or not at all. In 2013, for example, researchers from the New York University School of Medicine reported that lowered levels of the neurotransmitter norepinephrine transporter in a brain region that has a role in panic and stress was linked to PTSD. In this study, patients with PTSD showed 41 percent lower norepinephrine transporter levels than healthy control subjects.

Because many anxiety disorders involve an overly sensitive fear response, researchers believe that deficiencies in certain neurotransmitters that calm and inhibit the fear response are involved in the development of anxiety. For example, serotonin is a neurotransmitter that regulates feelings of well-being and affects appetite, sleep, mood, libido, and cognitive functions, which are all disturbed by anxiety. Some studies suggest that decreased levels of serotonin can lead to feelings of anxiety and depression, as well as the development of an anxiety disorder.

Other studies suggest that decreased levels of the neurotransmitter gamma-aminobutyric acid (GABA) may affect the development of anxiety. GABA acts as an inhibitory neurotransmitter; it slows down the activity of neurons in the central nervous system when it binds to a GABA receptor. Some researchers believe that one of GABA's roles is to control the fear and anxiety individuals experience when their neurons are overstimulated. In panic disorder, attacks may be caused by a defect or interference with GABA receptor function. Studies suggest that if GABA levels are low, a person may exhibit signs of stress and anxiety.

Scientists are also studying how hormones affect anxiety disorders. Hormones are chemicals that help the body's organs function. The stress hormone cortisol has been linked to anxiety. The body's adrenal glands release cortisol to activate the body's fight-or-flight response when a person feels stressed or threatened. Researchers have found that excess cortisol can cause both anxiety and depression and contribute to the chance of an anxiety attack. In addition, the hypothalamus, pituitary gland, and adrenal glands form a hormonal system that controls a person's mood. If the hormones produced by this system are not in balance, the system may become overexcited. The body and brain will perceive a situation as threatening even if it is not, which can lead to anxiety and feelings of apprehension, fear, and dread.

Scientists hope that learning more about how brain structure and chemistry influences fear and anxiety will lead to more effective

GABA (gamma-aminobutyric acid) receptors, pictured here in purple, change shape as the neurotransmitter binds to them. Since some scientists believe GABA helps control fear and anxiety, they theorize that a deficiency of this brain chemical or a defect in its functioning might contribute to heightened feelings of anxiety.

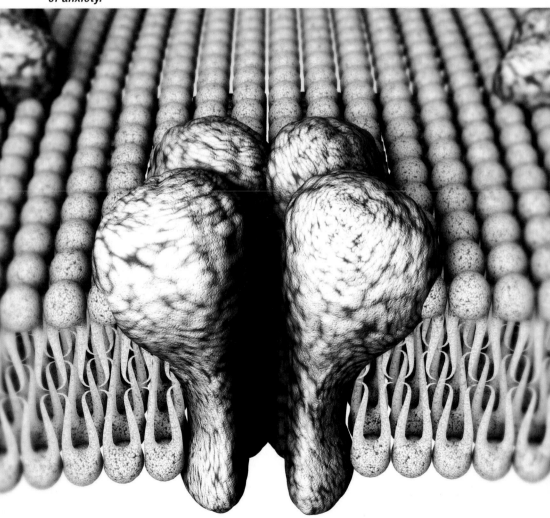

Family Environment

Genes may be one reason anxiety runs in families, but the family environment may be another influence. Some researchers believe that children can be conditioned to learn fears and phobias simply by watching the fearful reactions of parents and family members.

In the case of social anxiety disorder, parental behavior can increase a child's risk of anxiety. Parents diagnosed with social anxiety disorder typically show less warmth and affection toward their children, criticize them more often, and frequently express doubts that a child will be able to perform a task. Scientists say that these behaviors increase anxiety in children. If they are performed repeatedly over a long period, children become at greater risk of developing an anxiety disorder of their own. "Children with an inherited propensity to anxiety do not just become anxious because of their genes, so what we need are ways to prevent the environmental catalysts—in this case, parental behaviors—from unlocking the underlying genetic mechanisms responsible for the disease," says Golda Ginsburg, a researcher from Johns Hopkins Children's Center.

Quoted in Rick Nauert, "Parents' Anxiety Can 'Trickle Down' to Kids," PsychCentral, November 2, 2012. http://psychcentral.com.

treatments for anxiety disorders. "The ultimate aim is to understand the biology of mood and how groups of cells in the brain connect to produce our emotional behavior,"[21] says Jeremiah Cohen, an assistant professor at the Johns Hopkins Brain Science Institute in Baltimore.

Stress and Trauma

A person's life experiences can also be a factor in the development of an anxiety disorder. Everyone experiences stress at some point. Stress can come from relationships, work, school, and finances. Stress is common when a loved one dies or a job is lost. Even positive events such as the birth of a child or moving into a new house can cause stress. Stress is a normal part of life, yet everyone handles it differently. For some people stress can be a major contributor to anxiety or panic disorders and in some cases can trigger the onset of a disorder. In some cases a specific traumatic event can trigger an anxiety disorder, especially in people who are vulnerable to anxiety disorders because of other risk factors. War survivors and veterans are at a higher risk of developing PTSD, for example. According to the US Department of Veterans Affairs, approximately 30 percent of veterans from the Vietnam War will experience PTSD at some point in their lifetime, compared to 7 to 8 percent of the general population. Other traumatic events—such as being a victim of or witness to abuse or surviving a natural disaster—can trigger the onset of anxiety disorders in some people. A single traumatic experience can also trigger specific phobias, such as a fear of dogs or insects.

When stress continues over a period of months or years, it accumulates. This stress is more enduring than the normal, temporary stress of, say, moving to a new town or starting a new job. Cumulative stress may exist because of long-standing difficulties in a person's life, such as problems in a marriage or a difficult relationship with a parent. It may also be the accumulation of many life events, such as changing jobs, moving to a new city, having children, and so on. Although most people experience a major life event from time to time, having a series of several major events over a short period can cause stress to build up in a way that leads to chronic anxiety.

"The ultimate aim is to understand the biology of mood and how groups of cells in the brain connect to produce our emotional behavior."[21]

—Jeremiah Cohen, assistant professor at the Johns Hopkins Brain Science Institute in Baltimore, Maryland.

Some studies have found that high levels of stress during childhood may cause brain changes that make a person more likely to develop an anxiety disorder later in life. In 2012 scientists at the University of Wisconsin–Madison investigated whether high levels of family stress during infancy were linked to a higher risk of anxiety in teenage girls. In the study, researchers scanned the brains of fifty-seven participants and mapped the strength of connections between the amygdala and the prefrontal cortex. They discovered that female babies who lived in homes with stressed mothers were more likely to have higher cortisol levels at age four than babies whose mothers were not stressed.

In addition, brain scans revealed that girls with higher cortisol levels had less communication between brain areas associated with emotion regulation at age eighteen. Researchers also discovered that having both high cortisol levels at age four and reduced communication in brain areas associated with emotion regulation at age eighteen were associated with a higher risk of anxiety at age eighteen. These findings suggest that stress in early childhood and increased cortisol levels may have affected the girls' developing brains and increased their vulnerability to anxiety. "This will pave the way to better understanding of how the brain develops, and could give us insight into ways to intervene when children are young,"[22] says Richard Davidson, professor of psychology and psychiatry at the University of Wisconsin–Madison.

Researchers noted that boys in the study did not experience the same stress-related brain changes as girls. "Our findings raise questions on how boys and girls differ in the life impact of early stress," says Davidson. The differences in how stress affects the brain may be one reason why women have a higher risk of developing anxiety disorders. "We do know that women report higher levels of mood and anxiety disorders, and these sex-based differences are very pronounced, especially in adolescence,"[23] says Davidson.

Combination of Factors

It is unclear why some people are able to cope with worry and stress but others develop a mental illness. Most scientists believe that there is not a single cause of anxiety. Instead, they believe this group of mental illnesses develops from a combination of many factors. Psychiatrist Christos Dimitriou compares the causes of anxiety to a suspension bridge:

> Each support strut represents a gene, and the bridge represents your entire genetic loading. Everyday stressors are

represented by cars, and major stressors—divorce, bereavement, redundancy [losing one's job]—by lorries [trucks]. In the absence of any faulty genes, the bridge can handle all the traffic, but if there are a few faulty genes, the respective support struts will be weakened, and less able to cope with it, particularly the lorries.[24]

In other words, a person's ability to deal with stress depends on how his or her genes, brain structure, chemistry, stress, and other environmental factors interact with each other. Through research, scientists hope to better identify and understand the factors that influence a person's vulnerability to anxiety.

CHAPTER 3

What Is It like to Live with an Anxiety Disorder?

Anxiety disorders can be debilitating to those affected, as well as their families and friends. Anxiety can impair a person's ability to eat and sleep. It can damage relationships with family and friends and impair a person's ability to go to school or work. Having an anxiety disorder can also increase a person's risk of developing other mental health issues, substance abuse problems, and eating disorders. It may even increase a person's risk for suicide and suicidal thoughts.

Nicky Lidbetter runs two mental health charities in Britain yet says she remains critically challenged by the anxiety, panic attacks, and agoraphobia that she first began experiencing as a student. "I've achieved within the constraints the disorder has placed on me," she says. "But I continue to find it hard to travel. I live my life within a 50-mile radius." As her two children get older, travel, and live their own lives, Lidbetter has realized the crippling limitations of her disorder. "If I wanted to go and get them I wouldn't be able to, and that's awful really." As her children grow up, Nicky wonders how her anxiety will affect her relationship with them. In an attempt to overcome her fear, she rode a train for the first time in twenty-three years. "I didn't like it," she reports. "I thought: how long can I contain this anxiety before it completely overwhelms me?"[25]

Physical Effects

Although anxiety disorders are a mental illness, they also affect people physically. Some people experience muscle tension, backaches, and headaches. Others have gastrointestinal difficulties such as nausea and diarrhea. Some people feel dizzy and short of breath, whereas others experience heart palpitations; numbness in the arms, hands, or legs; and chest pains. Some have trouble sleeping, and others are constantly fatigued from anxious thoughts.

Claire Eastham, a twenty-six-year-old who suffers from anxiety, says that during her first year in college, her anxiety often made her sick. "That was when the overthinking started, the racing thoughts,"

Severe headaches are a common physical symptom of anxiety disorders. Over time, anxiety can lead to much more severe ailments, including heart disease and stroke.

she says. "Bad insomnia, lots of headaches, nausea. I would physically brace myself, hold my breath until my stomach began to hurt."[26] The physical effects of anxiety can become so disruptive that they drive a person to a medical professional. If a doctor cannot find a physical cause for the person's symptoms, they may be diagnosed with anxiety.

Over time, chronic stress and anxiety can have a lasting impact. Excess stress hormones constrict blood vessels and elevate blood pressure. Anxiety also affects a person's immune system, decreasing the number of white blood cells that fight bacteria and viruses. These changes can increase the risk of developing certain illnesses and make a person more susceptible to infections and other diseases.

One disease chronic anxiety has been linked to is heart disease. Research has shown that people with anxiety are more likely to experience sudden cardiac death. A 2010 study by Swedish researchers published in the *Journal of the American College of Cardiology* found that men diagnosed with anxiety in their late teens or early twenties were more than twice as likely to have heart disease or experience a heart attack later in life.

Another 2013 study, conducted by researchers at the University of Pittsburgh School of Medicine, linked anxiety to a higher risk of stroke. Participants who reported more severe anxiety symptoms had a 33 percent higher risk of stroke that those with the lowest levels of anxiety. Even small increases in anxiety appeared to increase a person's stroke risk. "Everyone has some anxiety now and then. But when it's elevated and/or chronic, it may have an effect on your vasculature [circulatory system] years down the road,"[27] says Maya Lambiase, a cardiovascular behavioral medicine researcher at the University of Pittsburgh School of Medicine.

> "Everyone has some anxiety now and then. But when it's elevated and/or chronic, it may have an effect on your vasculature [circulatory system] years down the road."[27]
>
> —Maya Lambiase, a cardiovascular behavioral medicine researcher at the University of Pittsburgh School of Medicine.

Emotional Impact

Anxiety disorders also affect a person's emotional state. Constant worrying can make a person feel unprotected and constantly on

Celebrities with Anxiety Disorders

According to Calm Clinic, a website by and for anxiety disorders, many successful actors, writers, sports stars, musicians, and politicians have been diagnosed with and treated for GAD. These include singer LeAnn Rimes, former president Abraham Lincoln, actor Johnny Depp, former football coach and NFL analyst John Madden, actress Emma Stone, model Kate Moss, singer Adele, actress Scarlett Johansson, and British singer George Michael. Several prominent celebrities have also been diagnosed with OCD, including comedian Howie Mandel, soccer star David Beckham, and singer Fred Durst.

guard. Chronic stress can make them feel overwhelmed by everyday situations. As a result, they may have trouble concentrating and may be irritable and restless.

Many sufferers are embarrassed by their illness and try to hide their symptoms from others. They may fear being judged as weak or strange. As a result, many people who struggle with anxiety feel misunderstood or alone. Team Canada Inline Hockey goalie Kendra Fisher says that she hid her struggle with anxiety for many years, not letting her teammates and coaches know the extent of her panic attacks. Doing so only made her illness more difficult to manage. "It was petrifying to be on the ice some nights," she says. "It wasn't something I allowed people to know I was going through, which made it more of a struggle."[28]

Effect on Relationships

According to an ADAA survey of people with GAD, anxiety often has the greatest impact on romantic relationships. Individuals with anxiety may become paranoid and suspicious. They may worry about their partner being unfaithful, not loving them, not caring enough, or other issues. Other times, people may look for constant reassurance from a partner that everything is all right. They may call a partner repeatedly to check in and make sure all is well. Anxiety may also cause a person to become impulsive, jump to conclusions, or make quick, ill-advised decisions. In many cases one partner's anxiety can leave both partners feeling frustrated and angry.

Having a partner with an anxiety disorder can be difficult. "Partners may find themselves in roles they do not want, such as the compromiser, the protector, or the comforter," says therapist Kate Thieda. She explains that they may have to take on extra responsibilities and give up certain activities, events, and places that trigger their partner's anxiety. "Partners of loved ones with anxiety may find themselves angry, frustrated, sad, or disappointed that their dreams for what the relationship was going to be have been limited by anxiety,"[29] says Thieda.

Relationships with partners, family, and friends suffer when people with anxiety adapt their behavior to avoid places and situations that may cause anxiety. They may make excuses to avoid going out or hurry to leave a place or situation that makes them feel anxious. When they do go out, some insist on sitting near doors or exits so they can leave in a hurry. They avoid buses and other forms of public transportation. Some may even cross the street to avoid encountering others. When these behaviors cause a person to repeatedly miss social and family events, it can strain relationships. "When my anxiety was at its worst, I had this really conflicted relationship with other people," says photographer John William Keedy. "I really wanted to be in contact with my friends and my family, but there was something physically just keeping me back from it. A friend would call, and I'd just stare at the phone. I'd really want to answer it, and I felt I couldn't. There was something keeping me from doing that."[30]

Anxiety can also cause problems at work and school. Symptoms can make it difficult to interact with coworkers and classmates. Individuals may turn down a promotion or opportunity because it involves anxiety-inducing travel or public speaking. They might make excuses to avoid office parties, staff lunches, meetings with coworkers, and school events. They may seek constant reassurance from co-

> "When my anxiety was at its worst, I had this really conflicted relationship with other people. I really wanted to be in contact with my friends and my family, but there was something physically just keeping me back from it."[30]
>
> —John William Keedy, a photographer who suffers from anxiety disorder.

workers, bosses, and teachers. They may have trouble meeting deadlines because they have a hard time concentrating and are constantly fatigued. As a result, anxiety disorder can significantly impair such people's work and school productivity. When anxiety becomes severe, they may be unable to leave home and may miss days of work or school.

For journalist Scott Neumyer, anxiety derailed his career as a teacher. After experiencing his first anxiety attack at a Bruce Springsteen concert one summer, Neumyer returned to school in September with no idea of the extent to which anxiety would impact his work. One day while he was substitute teaching, he had to take his students from the gym to the school's tiny, crowded library. "That slight change set me off completely," remembers Neumyer. "Halfway through class, as I sat at a table while the kids enjoyed a free period, I began sweating. . . . My eyes felt like they were bulging out of my head and my mouth was so dry you'd think I'd just eaten a boxful of chalk. I was out of my mind with anxiety."[31] When the bell rang to end the period, Neumyer ran out of the library and headed straight for the school's main office. He told the school secretary he was sick, and then he left the building. When he got home Neumyer buried himself under his bed covers and stayed there for hours. After that anxiety attack, Neumyer never returned to teaching. "I never worked another minute as a teacher, substitute or otherwise,"[32] he says.

Complications of Anxiety

Having an anxiety disorder can also lead to or worsen other mental health conditions. Depression is common in people with an anxiety disorder. In many cases the symptoms of depression and anxiety mirror and mask each other, making it difficult to distinguish between the two. Both disorders can cause agitation, insomnia, difficulty concentrating, and feelings of anxiety. For people with bipolar disorder, a mood disorder that causes depressive and manic states, anxiety can worsen symptoms.

Many people with anxiety disorders also have eating disorders. According to the ADAA, approximately two-thirds of people with eating disorders have an anxiety disorder at some point in their lives.

In addition, about 42 percent of people with an eating disorder had an anxiety disorder during childhood, before the onset of their eating disorder. The most common anxiety disorder that occurs with an eating disorder is OCD. People who have both OCD and an eating disorder often develop compulsions about food, such as weighing every piece of food or cutting it in specific ways. Scientists are unsure whether anxiety disorders, especially OCD, cause or increase a person's vulnerability to eating disorders or if the two types of disorders share common biological causes.

Substance Abuse

To deal with constant anxiety and fear, some people drink alcohol, smoke, or abuse other substances to relieve stress. Alcohol and other drugs affect receptors in the brain to temporarily reduce stress. Although a person may feel better in the short term, alcohol and other substances can make anxiety worse in the long run. Within a few hours of drinking, alcohol can actually increase anxiety and irritability.

In addition, repeated use of alcohol in social situations can lead to abuse. According to the ADAA, people with anxiety disorders are two to three times more likely to develop an alcohol or other substance abuse problem than people without anxiety. About 20 percent of Americans with an anxiety or mood disorder also have a substance abuse disorder. At the same time, about 20 percent of Americans with a substance abuse problem also have an anxiety or mood disorder.

PTSD has particularly been linked to substance abuse. The nightmares, panic attacks, and other symptoms of PTSD can be extremely upsetting. Many PTSD sufferers feel unable to cope with their symptoms and turn to alcohol or drugs to numb their pain and escape anxiety. According to the Foundations Recovery Network, an organization that treats people with substance addictions and mental health disorders, more than 50 percent of people with PTSD have an alcohol dependence, and more than 30 percent have a drug dependence.

Bob Curry is a Vietnam veteran who turned to alcohol to help him deal with PTSD after returning from the war. He ignored the signs of his disorder and tried to tough it out, using alcohol as a crutch. "If you have severe PTSD you're likely to self-medicate,"[33] explains Curry. Eventually, alcoholism took over his life. One night he was

Alcohol Dependence and Anxiety Disorders

Many people with anxiety disorders turn to alcohol to temporarily relieve their symptoms, and are therefore more likely to develop an alcohol use disorder (AUD) than people who do not have an anxiety disorder. For example, people with generalized anxiety disorder are three times more likely to have an AUD than people who have not been diagnosed with GAD.

Odds Ratio of the 12-Month Comorbidity Between Certain Anxiety Disorders and Alcohol Use

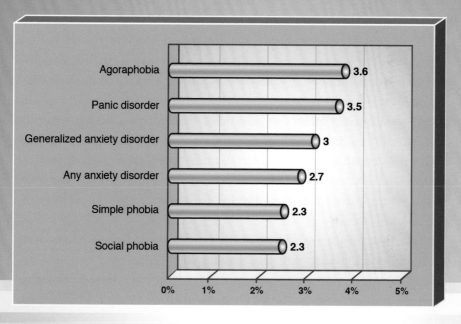

Source: Joshua P. Smith and Carrie L. Randall, "Anxiety and Alcohol Use Disorders," *Alcohol Research: Current Reviews* 34.4 (2012), May 1, 2015.

involved in a car accident that killed another person. Police arrested Curry and charged him with homicide by intoxicated use of a vehicle. He was found not guilty by reason of insanity and sent to an institution, where he received PTSD and substance abuse treatment. Today Curry works to help veterans and their families deal with PTSD and substance abuse.

People who have panic disorder may also turn to alcohol or drugs to calm themselves and reduce the fear of future panic attacks. Although using drugs and alcohol can temporarily relieve symptoms of panic disorder, repeated and frequent use can lead to a substance abuse problem. In some cases alcohol and drugs can intensify anxiety symptoms and trigger panic attacks, making the anxiety disorder more difficult to manage.

Suicide

For some people, living with constant fear and stress is unbearable. Feeling as if there is no hope of escape, they may consider suicide. According to the National Alliance on Mental Illness, the vast majority of people who commit suicide have been diagnosed with a mental illness such as anxiety disorder, depression, or bipolar disorder. Several anxiety disorders—including GAD, panic disorder, PTSD, social phobias, and OCD—increase a person's risk of suicide. A person's risk is even higher if he or she has both an anxiety disorder and a mood disorder such as depression. "More than 90 percent of those who commit suicide have a diagnosable illness such as clinical depression, and often in combination with anxiety or substance use disorders and other treatable mental disorders,"[34] says Mark Pollack, ADAA president.

In a 2013 study published in the journal *Depression and Anxiety*, researchers reviewed forty-two studies that researched the link between anxiety and suicidal behavior. The researchers learned patients with anxiety—particularly GAD, panic disorder, and PTSD—were more likely than those without anxiety to report suicidal thoughts. They were also more likely to have tried to commit suicide, completed suicide, or demonstrated suicidal behaviors.

Elizabeth Hawksworth, a Toronto-based writer, says that the pressure of college caused her anxiety to worsen and drove her to the brink of suicide. "My anxiety overwhelmed me," she remembers. "The smallest things were cause for catastrophe. I started sleeping all day; I refused to shower or brush my teeth. I skipped most of my classes and started skipping meals, too. By the time February rolled around, I was crashing and burning, badly." While Hawksworth was struggling to make it through each day, she felt ashamed and hid her anxiety from

Anxiety's History

Although some people associate anxiety with the modern problems of urban crowding, terrorism, and war, anxiety greatly predates the twenty-first century. Among the first people to recognize anxiety as a condition was Benedict de Spinoza, a Dutch philosopher who lived in the seventeenth century and noted that humanity seemed shackled by what he called "dread." Danish philosopher Søren Kierkegaard also discussed anxiety in his 1844 book *The Concept of Anxiety*, in which he described anxiety as a crisis of choice:

> Anxiety may be compared with dizziness. He whose eye happens to look down the yawning abyss becomes dizzy. But what is the reason for this? It is just as much in his own eye as in the abyss, for suppose he had not looked down. Hence, anxiety is the dizziness of freedom, which emerges when the spirit wants to posit the synthesis and freedom looks down into its own possibility, laying hold of finiteness to support itself.

Quoted in M. Jamie Ferreira, *Kierkegaard*. Hoboken, NJ: Wiley-Blackwell, 2009, pp. 83–84.

her family and friends. She felt depressed and guilty for failing her classes. "I felt like I was in a dark tunnel and could never get out. . . . It seemed as if my only option was to end everything and escape my parents' and friends' disappointment in me."[35]

One Thursday night, Hawksworth decided to end her life. She was prepared to go through with her plans, when a friend knocked on the door and interrupted her. "If my dorm floor had stayed quiet, I wouldn't be here today," she says. "I was saved that Thursday night by my best friend, knocking on my door. . . . I consider it a blessing, and the reason why I'm still alive today."[36] Afterward, Hawksworth realized she needed help and met with a counselor, who diagnosed her with GAD. With medication and therapy, Hawksworth learned to cope with her anxiety. Although she ended up dropping out of college, she eventually returned and graduated in 2006 with a degree in journalism.

Most suicides are preventable, according to the American Foundation for Suicide Prevention. Yet many people with anxiety disorders never seek help. "Sadly, many who are at risk for attempting suicide never receive the treatment they need because of stigma, lack of access to care, or lack of knowledge about their symptoms,"[37] says Karen Cassiday, managing director of the Anxiety Treatment Center in Deerfield, Illinois.

Living with a Phobia

It is common and traumatic to be cripplingly afraid of spiders, flying, or giving speeches. But many people are phobic of everyday objects that are difficult to avoid. For example, some people suffer from genuphobia, a fear of knees, which causes them to become nauseated, sweaty, and anxious in a situation that involves the knees or kneeling. Another documented phobia is trichophobia, a fear of hair. Trichophobics have strong physical reactions to seeing loose strands of hair on the floor, on clothing, and sometimes on people, as do pogonophobics—people who are afraid of beards.

> "Sadly, many who are at risk for attempting suicide never receive the treatment they need because of stigma, lack of access to care, or lack of knowledge about their symptoms."[37]
>
> —Karen Cassiday, managing director of the Anxiety Treatment Center in Deerfield, Illinois.

Daily life can also be trying for koumpounophobics, who fear buttons and similarly shaped objects like coins. Says one sufferer, who can barely muster the ability to say the word *button*: "If I touch one by accident, [for example] in a clothes shop, I can feel my heart suddenly jump and sometimes I feel like I'm going to be sick. If there are clothes lying around anywhere, I will always arrange them so that there are no buttons showing anywhere."[38] This particular sufferer avoids places like offices and nightclubs, where people typically wear clothes with buttons and where he would be expected to wear a button-down shirt.

Life is similarly difficult for euphobics (who fear good news); xerophobics (who fear dryness); omphalophobics (who fear belly buttons); frigophobics (who fear becoming too cold); papyrophobics

Phobias pertaining to everyday objects make life extremely challenging for sufferers. Koumpounophobics, for example, fear buttons, which are difficult to avoid on a day-to-day basis.

(who fear paper); haphophobics (who fear collarbones); and botano-phobics (who fear plants). Actress Christina Ricci has been diagnosed with this phobia, and says of plants, "They are dirty. I'm repulsed by the fact that there's a plant indoors. It just freaks me out."[39] When everyday objects that are encountered in homes, offices, schools, and other common places trigger intense physical revulsion and anxiety, true phobics find it very challenging to have a normal life.

Supporting a Loved One with Anxiety Disorder

Anxiety disorders affect a wide circle of people beyond the person diagnosed. Family, friends, and coworkers are among the many people who are impacted when someone in their lives is coping with an anxiety disorder. Supporting a person suffering from an anxiety disorder can be difficult, and partners, family, and friends often struggle with how best to help. Therapist Kate Thieda tells family and friends to avoid accommodating a person's anxiety, because by doing so they validate the fears and give the person little incentive to change.

This was the case with John, a twelve-year-old with OCD. His mother believed that accommodating his fears about contamination and gaining weight would help ease his anxiety. They thus did not go to restaurants or have any friends visit their home, because John feared they would bring germs. Yet John's anxiety only got worse. "Before I knew what accommodation was, I thought I was helping," says John's mother. "I was devastated to know I was feeding the OCD instead of helping John."[40]

Experts like Thieda say that family and friends should not limit their own lives to accommodate their loved one's anxiety. They should let their loved one know that from time to time, they are going to take care of their own wants and needs. When someone with an anxiety disorder decides to seek help, experts say that family and friends can best help by being supportive and encouraging.

Living with Anxiety Disorders

Anxiety disorder sufferers must learn to live with the many physical, emotional, and social effects of their illness. In spite of these challenges, many are able to live normal and productive lives. L.A. Nicholson is one person who has battled GAD for many years. She tried to commit suicide on two occasions. After her second attempt, Nicholson says she became determined to reclaim her life from anxiety. It was a long, hard process with many setbacks along the way, but she says it was worth the effort. "I not only got my life back, I gained a second career as an advocate for the mentally ill," she says. "I now work full time, raise my son, own my own home, and volunteer as an 'In Our Own Voice' presenter for the National Alliance on Mental Illness." Nicholson also wrote a book about her experiences, titled *What Doesn't Kill Us: My Battle with Anxiety*. "I firmly believe that if I can feel better, anyone can,"[41] she says.

CHAPTER 4

Can Anxiety Disorder Be Treated or Cured?

Many people may feel trapped by anxiety's fierce grip. Like other illnesses, however, anxiety disorders are treatable. The vast majority of people who receive treatment from a mental health professional experience an improvement in their symptoms.

Most anxiety disorders are treated with medication, psychotherapy, or a combination of the two. Some patients feel better within a few weeks or months, whereas others may need more than a year to see results. The type of anxiety disorder will inform what treatment is used. In addition, treatment may be longer and more complex if the patient suffers from multiple anxiety disorders or has other conditions, such as another mental illness or a substance abuse problem.

Even though anxiety disorders are highly treatable, the majority of sufferers do not receive adequate treatment. According to the ADAA, only about one-third of those with an anxiety disorder receive treatment. Left untreated, anxiety disorders can worsen and have severe consequences. People who suffer anxiety attacks may begin to avoid people, places, and situations they fear will trigger another attack. Untreated anxiety disorders can also lead to other mental illnesses, such as depression and substance abuse. Debilitating problems can develop at work, at school, and in relationships.

Diagnosis

The first step in treating an anxiety disorder it to accurately diagnose it. Many anxiety disorders have physical symptoms that can be confused with other ailments. In fact, it is often a physical symptom that drives people who are eventually diagnosed with an anxiety disorder to a doctor. Anxiety attacks mimic the symptoms of many acute disorders of the heart or lungs, including heart attacks and chest pain. As a result, many individuals with anxiety seek help because they think they have a life-threatening medical condition.

A doctor will carefully evaluate a patient to determine whether his or her symptoms stem from a physical problem. The doctor may perform a physical exam, order blood or urine tests, and ask detailed questions about a patient's symptoms and medical history.

If no physical cause can be found, the doctor or trained mental health professional may use a psychological questionnaire or otherwise interview the patient about symptoms, as well as take the patient's family and personal history of mental illness. Questions usually revolve around whether the patient has experienced a recent traumatic event, whether he or she drinks alcohol or uses drugs, and whether certain situations or places trigger feelings of anxiety. Some forms of anxiety, such as GAD, can be difficult to diagnose because sufferers do not have dramatic symptoms such as panic attacks or cannot trace their anxiety to a traumatic event. To aid diagnosis, the mental health professional may use various screening tests to determine the cause, type, severity, and frequency of anxiety.

If the patient is diagnosed with an anxiety disorder, the doctor will develop a personalized treatment plan. Most anxiety disorders are treated with a combination of talk therapy and medication. Certain lifestyle changes can also help anxiety symptoms, such as getting adequate exercise, getting enough sleep, and eating a healthy diet. Because anxiety is different for everyone, patients may need to try different types of treatments and medications until they find a combination that works best for them.

Former NFL player Ricky Williams struggled for years with social anxiety disorder. His fears increased during his professional football career. Pushed into the media spotlight, Williams became labeled as aloof and strange, especially because of the way he performed during interviews. Sometimes he answered reporters' questions while still wearing his football helmet. He frequently avoided fans. He even had difficulty interacting with his young daughter and leaving his house to do errands. No one knew it, but Williams acted so strangely because all of these interactions increased his anxiety.

Many Sufferers Do Not Seek Treatment

Although anxiety disorders are highly treatable, the majority of people suffering from them do not seek treatment. According to the National Institute of Mental Health (NIMH), only about one-third of adults with any anxiety disorder received treatment over a twelve-month period, and even fewer received treatment that is considered minimally adequate.

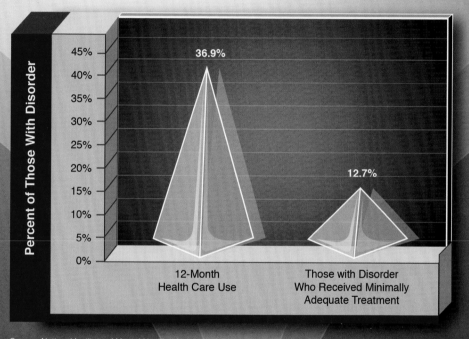

Source: National Institute of Mental Health, "Any Anxiety Disorder Among Adults." www.nimh.nih.gov.

On the suggestion of a friend, Williams finally decided to seek help from a mental health professional. After he was formally diagnosed with social anxiety disorder, Williams says he found hope for recovery. "I felt immense relief because it meant that there was a name for my suffering. I wasn't crazy or weird, like I thought for so many years," he says. Williams's treatment consisted of taking an antidepressant and going to regular therapy sessions. "Soon thereafter," he says, "I was able to start acting like the real Ricky Williams."[42]

Medication

Although medication does not cure anxiety disorders, it helps patients keep their symptoms under control while they learn to manage their anxiety in therapy. Medication can be a short-term or long-term treatment, depending on the severity of a patient's symptoms and if he or she suffers from another mental disorder or a substance abuse problem. The most common medications used to treat anxiety disorders are antidepressants, antianxiety drugs, and beta blockers.

"I felt immense relief because it meant that there was a name for my suffering. I wasn't crazy or weird, like I thought for so many years."[42]

—Ricky Williams, a former NFL player who has social anxiety disorder.

Initially developed to treat depression, antidepressants are effective for many anxiety disorders. Antidepressants work by adjusting brain chemicals such as serotonin to normal levels. Serotonin regulates feelings of well-being, and some studies suggest that decreased serotonin levels can lead to anxiety and depression. Medications that increase serotonin levels have been shown to reduce anxiety. Although these medications begin to affect brain chemistry immediately, it usually takes about four to six weeks for patients to feel relief.

Benzodiazepines are antianxiety medications that are used to manage anxiety. They help relax a patient, reduce muscle tension, and relieve anxiety's other physical symptoms. Because a patient can develop a tolerance to the medication and require increasingly higher doses in order to achieve the same effect, this type of medication is generally only used for a short time. Benzodiazepines such as Xanax and Valium are used to treat panic disorder, social anxiety disorder, and GAD, but they can have many side effects, including daytime drowsiness, dizziness, headache, and confusion.

Buspirone is a newer type of antianxiety medication that affects serotonin receptors in the brain, possibly stimulating the serotonin receptors on nerves and altering the chemical messages the nerves receive. It is used to treat GAD, although it is not effective for panic attacks. This medication generally has fewer side effects than benzodiazepines, although it must be taken for at least two weeks to be fully effective. Unlike benzodiazepines, it is not addictive and can be used in the event a patient also has a substance abuse problem.

Beta blockers are medications generally used to treat heart conditions. They are also sometimes prescribed to treat anxiety's physical symptoms, particularly those associated with social phobia. Beta blockers inhibit the nerves that stimulate the heart to beat faster. When a patient knows he or she will be in an anxiety-provoking situation—such as giving a speech—a doctor can prescribe a beta blocker to prevent the patient's heart rate from getting too rapid, which will help the patient stay calm.

Antidepressant drugs known as selective serotonin reuptake inhibitors can relieve anxiety symptoms. As this diagram illustrates, neurotransmitters such as serotonin (the yellow dots), which promotes feelings of well-being, travel between nerve cells across a space known as a synapse. The drugs work to facilitate this movement, ensuring normal serotonin levels in the brain.

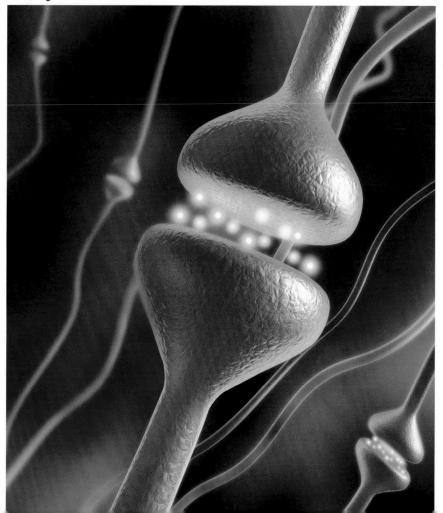

In some cases patients may decide to stop taking their medication without a doctor's approval. Some stop because they feel better and they think they no longer need it. Others stop because they do not like the associated side effects, which can include agitation, nausea, weight gain, and sexual dysfunction. Since many antianxiety medications take several weeks to work, patients may give up before the drug has had a chance to work. Patients are advised not to stop taking their medication without a doctor's approval. Several antianxiety drugs can cause withdrawal symptoms if they are not properly tapered (that is, slowly reduced) under a doctor's supervision.

Talk Therapy

Talk therapy, or psychotherapy, is a common way to treat anxiety disorders. During talk therapy, patients discuss with a trained mental health professional what may have caused their disorder and how they can best manage their symptoms. Talk therapy can occur in individual, group, or family sessions.

Cognitive behavioral therapy (CBT) is a common talk therapy used to treat anxiety disorders. CBT is based on the idea that people's thoughts influence their feelings and behaviors. The goal of CBT is to change how patients' thinking patterns support their anxiety and to teach them to respond positively to anxiety-producing situations. During CBT a therapist helps a patient learn to recognize anxious reactions and thoughts as they occur. The therapist also works with the patient to develop skills and techniques to reduce and cope with anxiety. CBT can help patients regain control of their reactions to stress and reduce the feeling of helplessness that often accompanies an anxiety disorder.

Initial talk therapy treatment generally occurs over a twelve- to twenty-week period. Claire Eastham reports that CBT helped her manage her panic attacks. "I had 10 sessions," she says, "and it changed everything." She says it felt good to talk about what she was feeling with someone who understood and did not dismiss her feelings as something she could just turn off like a faucet. Therapy also gave her the tools she needed to manage her anxiety. "I still have bad days, but at least now I have a strategy,"[43] she says.

Exposure Therapy

Because anxiety disorders are a chronic illness, relapse is common, even after successful short-term therapy. Therefore, some patients require long-term or intensive therapy of at least a year to relieve their anxiety symptoms. One form of CBT called exposure therapy is a specific technique used to reduce a patient's fear and anxiety responses over time. Patients are gradually exposed to a situation or object that causes them anxiety.

Often, the therapist will go with the person to the feared situation for support and guidance. As the exposure is repeated over time, the stimulating situation eventually loses its effect. "Overcoming fear is about learning to predict and, when possible, control the feared object or situation," explains Katherina Hauner, a neurologist at Northwestern University Feinberg School of Medicine who has studied the effect of exposure therapy on fear. "One learns how to approach the feared object or situation, so that it is no longer unpredictable and uncontrollable, which makes it far less threatening."[44] She says that even a single session of exposure therapy can eliminate the disabling fear that some patients experience.

Exposure therapy is effective for several anxiety disorders, particularly OCD and specific phobias. For example, a patient with OCD who fears germs may be asked to get his or her hands dirty and then wait increasing amounts of time before washing them. A patient with social phobia may spend increasing amounts of time at the mall or a crowded movie theater. Patients with PTSD may be encouraged recall their traumatic event in a safe place, which can reduce the fear it produces. To help patients cope with the anxiety produced during exposure therapy, therapists teach deep breathing and other relaxation techniques.

> "Overcoming fear is about learning to predict and, when possible, control the feared object or situation. One learns how to approach the feared object or situation, so that it is no longer unpredictable and uncontrollable, which makes it far less threatening."[44]
>
> —Katherina Hauner, a neurologist at Northwestern University Feinberg School of Medicine.

Brain Imaging to Tailor Treatment

For patients with social anxiety disorder, doctors generally prescribe psychotherapy and medications. It is difficult, however, to predict how patients will respond to treatment. Doctors have turned to brain imaging to help.

In 2013 researchers at the Massachusetts Institute of Technology reported that brain imaging can identify neuromarkers that predict whether traditional treatments such as CBT will work for a specific patient. The study used fMRIs to scan the brains of patients with social anxiety disorder while the patients viewed scenes and angry and neutral faces. Patients whose brains showed more activity in response to facial images responded best to CBT. In the scans, these patients' brains lit up with activity the most, especially in two areas near the back of the brain that process sight. Doctors hope they will be able to use such imaging techniques to customize treatments to best benefit patients.

Since patients' problems stem from all different sources and experiences, exposure therapy is customized specifically for them.

The first steps of exposure may be difficult for patients because they do not know what to expect and their fear levels peak. Eventually, though, patients' fears subside over subsequent sessions. "As long as the patient is motivated to overcome their fear, and they slowly approach the feared situation rather than escaping from it or avoiding it, they will eventually succeed," says Hauner. She cautions that the key to exposure therapy is to increase stress at a reasonable pace, progressing but not overwhelming the patient. The steps should create a moderate level of anxiety in the patient; anything more may cause the patient to quit or completely avoid the situation. "The most important thing is to keep engaged with the feared situation and not avoid it, even though it can be uncomfortable and difficult at first,"[45] she says.

Most people are able to reduce or eliminate their symptoms within several months of appropriate therapy. Many people even notice improvement within a few sessions. According to the experts at the University of North Carolina Anxiety and Stress Disorders Clinic, more than 60 percent of patients who undergo CBT experience substantial improvement in symptoms. Typically, this improvement can be seen in twelve to twenty treatment sessions.

Complementary Treatments

In addition to medication and talk therapy, stress and relaxation techniques can temporarily reduce anxiety symptoms. Relaxation techniques use muscle relaxation and mental visualization to create a calm feeling. Breathing techniques can help patients control their breathing, which can lessen uncomfortable symptoms such as dizziness, shortness of breath, and a lump in the throat. During a panic attack, a person may begin to hyperventilate. Using practiced, controlled breathing at the outset may help prevent a full-blown attack.

Techniques such as meditation, yoga, and acupuncture may also relieve anxiety symptoms. "For someone with anxiety, it sometimes feels like their mind is like a hamster on a wheel—constantly running, but not really getting anywhere," says Tom Corboy, executive director of the OCD Center of Los Angeles. Through meditation, however, patients can learn to quiet their brains. "Ultimately, meditation helps us slow down, get perspective, and think more objectively and with less knee-jerk reactivity. And *that* helps us be less anxious,"[46] Corboy adds.

> "Ultimately, meditation helps us slow down, get perspective, and think more objectively and with less knee-jerk reactivity. And *that* helps us be less anxious."[46]
>
> —Tom Corboy, founder and executive director of the OCD Center of Los Angeles.

Gayathri Ramprasad is a mental health advocate who struggled with anxiety and depression until meditation helped her cope. "When a medical resident at the hospital suggested I try transcendental meditation to manage my anxiety and depression, I did,"[47] she reports. She remembers learning how to meditate, sitting cross-legged on a carpet in her friend's home. At first, Ramprasad had trouble relaxing enough to keep her eyes closed and her breath steady, and her thoughts continued to race. Over time, though, she learned how to quiet her mind and body. "I discovered an oasis of energy, creativity, and restful calm," she says. "In time, meditation offered me a sacred space to reflect on my life, and taught me to become an observer of my thoughts and emotions instead of getting entangled in them."[48] Eventually, practicing meditation daily helped Ramprasad regulate her emotions and control her anxiety.

Yoga can also help with anxiety. Yoga combines physical poses, breathing exercises, and mindful meditation. Studies suggest that practicing yoga can help reduce heart rate and blood pressure and can relieve anxiety and depression. In a 2012 study, researchers from Brigham and Women's Hospital in Boston and Harvard Medical School reported that teens who participated in yoga during gym class showed significant improvement with anxiety and mood problems, compared to teens who did not have yoga during gym. According to Elliott Watlington, who teaches yoga to athletic teams at Wake Forest University, "I can see the transformation. . . . When my students struggle with anxiety or depression and then focus that energy on their yoga mat instead, that's just a really beautiful thing. They are calmer and more content."[49]

> "When my students struggle with anxiety or depression and then focus that energy on their yoga mat instead, that's just a really beautiful thing. They are calmer and more content."[49]
>
> —Elliott Watlington, a yoga instructor for the athletic teams at Wake Forest University.

Yoga may also reduce anxiety by increasing GABA levels in the brain. GABA is an inhibitory neurotransmitter that slows down neurons to calm fear and anxiety. In 2007 researchers at the Boston University School of Medicine reported that in their study of experienced yoga practitioners, GABA activity increased 27 percent after an hour-long yoga session, compared to a control group of participants who read quietly for the hour. In 2010 the researchers followed up the study and compared the effects of yoga and walking on a treadmill. They found that yoga practitioners reported improved anxiety and mood, compared to the walking participants. And MRIs of study participants' brains showed an increase in GABA for the yoga practitioners, compared to the walkers. "Yoga influences key elements of the brain in similar ways to antidepressants and psychotherapy," says P.

Two girls practice yoga in a park. Yoga and meditation can both relieve anxiety because they serve to quiet the racing thoughts that characterize the disorder.

Murali Doraiswamy, a neuroscientist from Duke University. "If the promise of yoga on the mind-body was found in a drug, it would be the best selling medication worldwide."[50]

Acupuncture is another alternative way to treat anxiety. Acupuncture is the ancient Chinese practice of inserting needles into the body at specific points to alleviate pain and treat many physical, mental, and emotional conditions. Acupuncture is based on the theory that energy flows through the body and illness occurs when something blocks its flow. The placement of acupuncture needles into certain points on the body is believed to restore proper energy flow.

Daniel Hsu, an acupuncture practitioner, explains that acupuncture can cause the body's nervous system to produce painkilling chemicals, trigger the body's natural ability to self-heal, and stimulate the part of the brain that controls emotions, including anxiety. In this way patients feel more balanced. Acupuncture can treat a variety of illnesses, including anxiety disorders. "We're constantly under stress and pressure to perform, which can bring on disease and other serious health issues," Hsu says. "Acupuncture is great for maintenance. It helps a long life become a better-quality life."[51]

Lifestyle Changes

Certain lifestyle changes can also reduce stress and anxiety symptoms. Regular exercise, adequate nutrition, and getting enough

Love Hormone to Treat Anxiety

Many people with anxiety disorders control their symptoms with medication. Because current antidepressant and antianxiety medications do not work for everyone, scientists are investigating new medical treatment with oxytocin, a brain hormone. Oxytocin is sometimes called the love hormone because it is able to reduce stress and encourage social behavior such as trust, empathy, and taking social risks. Studies have shown that oxytocin can make the amygdala react with less activity in response to pictures of threatening or fearful faces.

In a 2013 paper, researchers from the University of Illinois and Cambridge University reported on their study that investigated how oxytocin affects the brain in people with anxiety disorder. In the study, they showed participants pictures of fearful faces while scanning their brains using fMRI. In participants with GAD, the amygdala communicated significantly less with other parts of the brain, compared to participants who did not have GAD. The less connected the amygdala was to other brain areas, the higher the participant's anxiety levels. The researchers found that the oxytocin increased the connection of the amygdala to other brain regions in anxiety patients. They hope that further studies will improve understanding of how oxytocin can be used to treat people with anxiety disorders.

sleep all enhance general health and help build up resistance to stress. Exercise is a proven way to reduce and manage stress because it releases chemicals called endorphins into the brain, which naturally lift mood and boost energy. Aerobic exercise can decrease overall tension, elevate and stabilize mood, and improve sleep and self-esteem.

Managing stress can also reduce the risk and impact of anxiety disorders. Setting aside personal time away from the distractions of work and family can help a person recharge and lower stress. Some people use favorite activities such as art, music, writing, and volunteering as ways to relax and relieve stress. Following the advice of a friend, author Tracy Shawn decided to tackle her anxiety by writing a novel, which featured a protagonist who also struggled with anxiety disorder. After several months of writing, Shawn realized that the writing process had eased her symptoms. "The anxiety had decreased so much that it no longer felt like a major disease in which I had to battle, but rather like an annoying allergy I merely had to tend to from time to time,"[52] she says. The more she wrote about her character learning to overcome anxiety, the more her own fear and worry decreased.

Finally, managing anxiety involves getting support. Support can come from family, friends, a doctor, or a therapist. Diagnosed with GAD, twenty-three-year-old Stacy Gregg says that the support of her best friend, Stephanie, has helped her successfully manage her anxiety. Stephanie "has always been there for me and never passes judgment. After patiently listening to me, she could always ease my fears and anxiety,"[53] says Gregg. Many people find that joining a support group and meeting others who have had similar experiences can help them feel less alone and learn to better manage their disorder.

Living Successfully with Anxiety

Anxiety disorders are serious mental illnesses that can significantly impact a person's entire life. Many people who seek appropriate treatment with a qualified mental health professional are able to learn to manage their anxiety and lead productive and fulfilling lives. One of them is Rachel, a high school teen with GAD. Dealing with anxiety has been among the greatest challenges of her life, but her experience has made her stronger and more confident. "I learned that living a life of fear is not living at all," she says. "There is no problem that I can't handle." Rachel can now take risks and face challenges directly, instead of being ruled by fear. "The rewards of trying, whether I succeed or not, are always better than letting my worries run my life or wondering what would have happened if I'd only had the courage to try,"[54] she says.

SOURCE NOTES

Introduction: Gripped by Fear

1. Richard Lucas, "Anxiety, You're Not the Boss of Me," CNN, February 11, 2013. www.cnn.com.

2. Lucas, "Anxiety, You're Not the Boss of Me."

3. Lucas, "Anxiety, You're Not the Boss of Me."

4. Lucas, "Anxiety, You're Not the Boss of Me."

Chapter 1: What Is Anxiety Disorder?

5. Scott Stossel, "Surviving Anxiety," *Atlantic*, January/February 2014. www.theatlantic.com.

6. Kat Kinsman, "Living with Anxiety, Searching for Joy," CNN, January 8, 2014. www.cnn.com.

7. Kinsman, "Living with Anxiety, Searching for Joy."

8. Lee Kynaston, "Panic Attacks Are Nothing to Be Ashamed Of," *Telegraph* (London), December 5, 2013. www.telegraph.co.uk.

9. David Morris, "After PTSD, More Trauma," *Opinionator* (blog), *New York Times*, January 17, 2015. http://opinionator.blogs.ny times.com.

10. P.K. Phillips, "My Story of Survival: Battling PTSD," Anxiety and Depression Association of America. www.adaa.org.

11. Quoted in Elizabeth Landau, "Who's Afraid of Snakes, Spiders, Vomit?," CNN, June 15, 2010. www.cnn.com.

Chapter 2: What Causes Anxiety Disorder?

12. Edmund Bourne, *The Anxiety and Phobia Workbook*, 6th ed. Oakland, CA: New Harbinger, 2015. Kindle edition.

13. Quoted in National Institute of Mental Health, "Findings in Rats Could Explain Women's Increased Vulnerability to Disorders," transcript, August 9, 2010. www.nimh.nih.gov.

14. Quoted in Florida State University, "Why Does Anxiety Target Women More? FSU Researcher Awarded $1.8M Grant to Find Out," Newswise, September 1, 2010. www.newswise.com.

15. Quoted in Taylor Clark, "Nervous Nellies," *Slate*, April 20, 2011. www.slate.com.

16. Quoted in University of Chicago Medicine, "Genetic Analysis Reveals Novel Insights into the Genetic Architecture of Obsessive-Compulsive Disorder, Tourette Syndrome," October 24, 2013. www.uchospitals.edu.

17. Quoted in Johns Hopkins Medicine, "Researchers Identify Genetic Marker Linked to OCD," May 13, 2014. www.hopkins medicine.org.

18. Quoted in Christopher Bergland, "The Size and Connectivity of the Amygdala Predicts Anxiety," *Psychology Today*, November 20, 2013. www.psychologytoday.com.

19. Quoted in University of Cambridge, "Obsessive Compulsive Disorder Linked to Brain Activity," ScienceDaily, July 18, 2008. www.sciencedaily.com.

20. Quoted in Katie Charles, "Obsessive-Compulsive Is a Leading Cause of Disability Worldwide, with Causes Not Fully Understood," *New York Daily News*, July 21, 2013. www.nydailynews .com.

21. Quoted in Haroon Siddique, "Serotonin Map of Brain Could Lead to Better Targeted Antidepressants," *Guardian* (Manchester), January 5, 2015. www.theguardian.com.

22. Quoted in University of Wisconsin–Madison, "Early Stress May Sensitize Girls' Brains for Later Anxiety," November 11, 2012. www.news.wisc.edu.

23. Quoted in University of Wisconsin–Madison, "Early Stress May Sensitize Girls' Brains for Later Anxiety."

24. Quoted in Rachel Cooke, "Living with Anxiety: Britain's Silent Epidemic," *Guardian* (Manchester), September 14, 2013. www .theguardian.com.

Chapter 3: What Is It like to Live with Anxiety Disorder?

25. Quoted in Cooke, "Living with Anxiety."

26. Quoted in Cooke, "Living with Anxiety."

27. Quoted in American Heart Association, "Anxiety Linked to Higher Long-Term Risk of Stroke," ScienceDaily, December 19, 2013. www.sciencedaily.com.

28. Quoted in Scott Neumyer, "I Am Royce White," SB Nation, May 9, 2013. www.sbnation.com.

29. Quoted in Margarita Tartakovsky, "How to Support an Anxious Partner," Psych Central, March 27, 2013. http://psychcentral .com.

30. Quoted in Maanvi Singh, "A Life of Anxiety Documented," NPR, August 12, 2014. www.npr.org.

31. Neumyer, "I Am Royce White."

32. Neumyer, "I Am Royce White."

33. Quoted in Stephanie Graham and Courtny Gerrish, "Saving Our Soldiers: The Fight Against PTSD," News Radio 620 WTMJ, February 18, 2013. www.620wtmj.com.

34. Quoted in Anxiety and Depression Association of America, "Suicide." www.adaa.org.

35. Elizabeth Hawksworth, "College Drove Me to the Brink of Suicide," *Washington Post*, September 18, 2014. www.washington post.com.

36. Hawksworth, "College Drove Me to the Brink of Suicide."

37. Quoted in Anxiety and Depression Association of America, "Suicide."

38. Quoted in News.com.au, "Phobias So Weird They'll Scare You," October 23, 2012. www.news.com.au.

39. Quoted in News.com.au, "Phobias So Weird They'll Scare You."

40. Quoted in Linda Spiro, "Kids and OCD: The Parents' Role in Treatment," Child Mind Institute, February 26, 2013. www .childmind.org.

41. L.A. Nicholson, "What Doesn't Kill Us: My Battle with Generalized Anxiety Disorder," Anxiety and Depression Association of America. www.adaa.org.

Chapter 4: Can Anxiety Disorder Be Treated or Cured?

42. Quoted in Leslie Anderson, "Ricky Williams: A Story of Social Anxiety Disorder," Anxiety and Depression Association of America. www.adaa.org.

43. Quoted in Cooke, "Living with Anxiety."

44. Quoted in Elizabeth Kuster, "Conquering Fear: How Exposure Therapy Works," *Huffington Post*, September 28, 2012. www.huff ingtonpost.com.

45. Quoted in Kuster, "Conquering Fear."

46. Quoted in Margarita Tartakovsky, "How Meditation Helps Anxiety," Psych Central, November 12, 2014. http://psychcentral .com.

47. Gayathri Ramprasad, "Depression, Anxiety: What Worked for Me," CNN, March 5, 2014. www.cnn.com.

48. Ramprasad, "Depression, Anxiety."

49. Quoted in Shelley Roupas, "Yoga Used to Relieve Anxiety and Depression," Fox8 News, April 6, 2015. http://myfox8.com.

50. Quoted in Roupas, "Yoga Used to Relieve Anxiety and Depression."

51. Quoted in Maura Hohman, "Why Acupuncture Works for Anxiety Relief," EverydayHealth.com, August 21, 2014. www.every dayhealth.com.

52. Tracy Shawn, "How Writing Helped Me Conquer Real-Life Anxiety," Psych Central, March 23, 2014. http://psychcentral.com.

53. Stacy Gregg, "Now I'm in Control," Anxiety and Depression Association of America. www.adaa.org.

54. Rachel, "Anxiety: Rachel's Story," TeensHealth, October 2013. http://teenshealth.org.

ORGANIZATIONS TO CONTACT

American Academy of Child & Adolescent Psychiatry (AACAP)

3615 Wisconsin Ave. NW
Washington, DC 20016
phone: (202) 966-7300
fax: (202) 966-2891
website: www.aacap.org

The AACAP is a national professional medical association dedicated to treating and improving the quality of life for children, adolescents, and families affected by mental, behavioral, or developmental disorders.

American Foundation for Suicide Prevention (AFSP)

120 Wall St., 29th Floor
New York, NY 10005
phone: (888) 333-2377
fax: (212) 363-6237
e-mail: info@afsp.org
website: www.afsp.org

The AFSP is the leading national not-for-profit organization dedicated to understanding and preventing suicide through research, education, and advocacy and to reaching out to people with mental disorders and those impacted by suicide.

American Psychiatric Association

1000 Wilson Blvd., Suite 1825
Arlington, VA 22209
phone: (888)-357-7924
e-mail: apa@psych.org
website: www.psychiatry.org

The American Psychiatric Association has more than thirty-eight thousand US and international member physicians working together to ensure humane care and effective treatment for all persons with mental disorders. It publishes many books and journals, including the widely read *American Journal of Psychiatry*.

American Psychological Association

750 First St. NE
Washington, DC 20002-4242
phone: (800) 374-2721
e-mail: public.affairs@apa.org
website: www.apa.org

The American Psychological Association represents more than 148,000 American psychologists, who are professionals who study and treat human behavior. Their website features information about psychology topics, including anxiety disorders, and links to many publications.

Anxiety Disorders Association
of America (ADAA)

8701 Georgia Ave., Suite #412
Silver Spring, MD 20910
phone: (240) 485-1001
fax: (240) 485-1035
website: www.adaa.org

The ADAA is a national nonprofit organization that works to promote the prevention, treatment, and cure of anxiety, depression, OCD, PTSD, and related disorders. It also strives to improve the lives of all those who suffer from them through education, practice, and research. The ADAA website features information, news, and resources for those living with anxiety disorders.

Association for Behavioral and
Cognitive Therapies

305 Seventh Ave., 16th Floor
New York, NY 10001

phone: (212) 647-1890
fax: (212) 647-1865
website: www.abct.org

This association represents therapists who provide CBT for people who suffer from many types of mental illnesses, including anxiety disorders. The association's website features fact sheets on mental illnesses.

Freedom from Fear

308 Seaview Ave.
Staten Island, NY 10305
phone: (718) 351-1717 ext. 20
e-mail: help@freedomfromfear.org
website: www.freedomfromfear.org

Freedom from Fear is a national not-for-profit mental health advocacy association. The organization's mission is to provide a positive impact on the lives of all those affected by anxiety, depression, and related disorders through advocacy, education, research, and community support.

International OCD Foundation

18 Tremont St., Suite 903
Boston, MA 02108
phone: (617) 973-5801
website: www.ocfoundation.org

The International OCD Foundation is a not-for-profit organization of people with OCD and related disorders as well as their families, friends, professionals, and others. The foundation strives to educate the public and professionals about OCD, support research of OCD causes and effective treatments, and improve access to resources for people with OCD.

Mental Health America

2000 N. Beauregard St., 6th Floor
Alexandria, VA 22311
phone: (800) 969-6642

fax: (703) 684-5968
website: www.mentalhealthamerica.net

Mental Health America is an advocacy group for people with mental illnesses and their families. The organization's website features many resources, including fact sheets on anxiety disorders, information on finding support groups, and ways to help support research and funding for mental illnesses.

National Alliance on Mental Illness (NAMI)
3803 N. Fairfax Dr., Suite 100
Arlington, VA 22203
phone: (703) 524-7600
fax: (703) 524-9094
website: www.nami.org

The NAMI is an advocacy group for people with mental illnesses and includes local chapters in every state. The alliance offers education programs and services for individuals, family members, health care providers, and the public. The NAMI also serves as a voice in Washington, DC, and state houses across the country for Americans with mental illness.

National Institute of Mental Health (NIMH)
6001 Executive Blvd.
Bethesda, MD 20892-9663
phone: (866) 615-6464
e-mail: nimhinfo@nih.gov
website: www.nimh.nih.gov

The NIMH is the federal government's chief funding agency for mental health research in America. The institute's website provides fact sheets and information about mental illness, including anxiety disorders, and the latest science news and research on these illnesses.

FOR FURTHER RESEARCH

Books

Noah Berlatsky, *Mental Illness*. Detroit, MI: Greenhaven, 2013.

Sheri Bloom and Suzanne Mouton-Odum, *Out of the Rabbit Hole: A Road Map to Freedom from OCD*. Houston, TX: Wonderland, 2013.

Shirley Brinkerhoff, *Anxiety Disorders*. Broomhall, PA: Mason Crest, 2014.

Dale Carlson and Michael Bower, *Out of Order: Young Adult Manual of Mental Illness and Recovery*. Branford, CT: Bick, 2013.

Carrie Iorizzo, *Anxiety and Phobias*. St. Catherines, ON: Crabtree, 2014.

Hayley Leitch and Veronica Clark, *Coming Clean: Living with OCD*. London: Blake, 2014.

Christopher Willard, *Mindfulness for Teen Anxiety: A Workbook for Overcoming Anxiety at Home, at School, and Everywhere Else*. Oakland, CA: New Harbinger, 2014.

Internet Sources

Richard Lucas, "Anxiety, You're Not the Boss of Me," CNN, February 11, 2013. www.cnn.com/2013/02/11/health/anxiety-first-person-irpt.

National Alliance on Mental Illness, "Anxiety Disorders Fact Sheet," April 2012. www2.nami.org/factsheets/anxietydisorders_factsheet.pdf.

National Alliance on Mental Illness, "Panic Disorder Fact Sheet," February 2013. www2.nami.org/factsheets/panicdisorder_factsheet.pdf.

National Institute of Mental Health, "Panic Disorder: When Fear Overwhelms," 2013. www.nimh.nih.gov/health/publications/panic-disorder-when-fear-overwhelms/index.shtml.

Scott Neumyer, "I Am Royce White," SB Nation, May 9, 2013. www.sbnation.com/longform/2013/5/9/4312406/royce-white-living-and-working-with-anxiety-disorder.

New York Times, "Generalized Anxiety Disorder," March 11, 2013. www.nytimes.com/health/guides/disease/generalized-anxiety-disorder/in-depth-report.html.

Scott Stossel, "Surviving Anxiety," *Atlantic*, January/February 2014. www.theatlantic.com/magazine/archive/2014/01/surviving_anxiety/355741/?single_page=true.

Websites

Beyond OCD (http://beyondocd.org). This website provides information and resources about OCD, a type of anxiety disorder.

Dana Foundation (www.dana.org). This website provides information about the brain and brain research, including research on the brain and mental illness.

Teen Mental Health (www.teenmentalhealth.org). This website provides information and resources for teens to learn about mental health issues.

INDEX

cognitive behavioral therapy (CBT), 56–58, 59

Cohen, Jeremiah, 34

complementary treatments, 59–62, **61**

complications. *See* co-occurring disorders

Concept of Anxiety, The (Kierkegaard), 47

co-occurring disorders
  depression, 43
    eating disorders, 43–44
    mental health conditions, 43
    substance abuse, 44–46, **45**

Corboy, Tom, 59

cortisol, 30–31, 32–33, 36

Craske, Michelle, 24

culture as cause, 24–25

Curry, Bob, 44–45

danger, natural response to, 9

Davidson, Richard, 36

depression
  as co-occurring disorder, 43
  heredity and risk, 26–27
  suicide and, 46

Depression and Anxiety (journal), 46

diagnosis, 25, 40, 51–53

Dimitriou, Christos, 36–37

Doraiswamy, P. Murali, 60–61

Eastham, Claire, 39–40, 56

eating disorders, 43–44

effects
  emotional, 40–41
  on friends, family, and coworkers, 49–50
  physical, 6–7, 17, 38–40
  on relationships, 41–43
  suicide, 46–48

emetophobia, 20

emotional effects, 40–41

emotions, regulation by amygdala of, 28

endorphins, 63

environment as cause, 24–25, 34

exercise, 62–63

exposure therapy, 57–58

family, effects on, 49–50

family environment, 34, 42

Fanselow, Michael, 26

fear
  amygdala regulation of, 28–29
  as conditioned response, 34

exposure therapy and, 57

free-floating, in GAD, 15

irrational, 9–10

neurotransmitter deficiencies, 32

as part of panic attacks, 16, 17

See also phobias; specific phobias

"fear center" of brain, 28–29

fight-or-flight stress response, 9, 32

Fisher, Kendra, 41

Florida State University, 24

Foundations Recovery Network, 44

friends
  effects on, 49–50
  support from, 63

functional magnetic resonance imaging (fMRI), 29, 31, 58, 62

gamma-aminobutyric acid (GABA), 32, 33, 60–61

gender
  development of anxiety disorder and, 12
    environmental and cultural influences, 24–25, 35–36
    GAD, 14
    hormones, 23–24, 36
  likelihood of diagnosis and, 25
  OCD and, 15

generalized anxiety disorder (GAD)
  alcohol use and, 45
  amygdala and oxytocin, 62
  celebrities with, 41
  diagnosis of, 52
  effect on romantic relationships, 41–42
  heredity and risk, 26
  overview of, 14–15
  suicide risk and, 46
  treatment for, 54–55

genuphobia, 48

Ginsburg, Golda, 34

Gregg, Stacy, 63

Grice, Dorothy, 31

Harvard Medical School, 60

Hauner, Katherina, 57, 58

Hawksworth, Elizabeth, 46–47

heart disease, 40

heredity, 26–28

hippocampus, 29–31

Hispanics and development of anxiety disorders, 12–13

PICTURE CREDITS

ABOUT THE AUTHOR

Carla Mooney is the author of many books for young adults and children. She lives in Pittsburgh, Pennsylvania, with her husband and three children.